Visions of Greatness

Volume III

Visions of Greatness

VOLUME III

A COLLECTION OF INSPIRATIONAL STORIES

RABBI YOSEF WEISS

C.I.S. PUBLISHERS

New York • London • Jerusalem

Copyright ©1997

All rights reserved.
This book, or any part thereof,
may not be reproduced in any
form whatsoever without the express
written permission of the copyright holder.

Published and distributed
in the U.S. and overseas by:
C.I.S. Publishers and Distributors
180 Park Avenue, Lakewood, New Jersey 08701
Tel: (732) 905-3000   •   Fax: (732) 367-6666

Cover design: Deenee Cohen
Typography and Book Design: Meira Hochster

ISBN 1-56062-318--7 hard cover
1-56062-319-5 soft cover

The C.I.S. Publisher's Judaica Catalogue
is available upon request.
Inquiries about membership in the
C.I.S. Publisher's Privileged Readers Membership Club
should be directed to:
180 Park Avenue, Lakewood, New Jersey 08701
or call (732) 905-3000, fax (732) 367-6666

PRINTED IN THE UNITED STATES OF AMERICA

VOLUME III

הסכמת הרב משה אהרן שטרן שליט״א

KAMENITZER YESHIVA
"Knesseth Beth Isaac"
Jerusalem

ישיבה קמניץ
"כנסת בית יצחק"
ירושלים

Rabbi M.A. Stern
-Dean of Students

הרב משה אהרן שטרן
-מנהל רוחני

בס״ד ל׳ תמוז שנת

לכבוד ידידי היקר והנעלה הרב ר׳ יוסף יונה
ווייס שליט״א

שמחתי לשמוע שאתה עומד
כדאי להוציא לאור ספר שיש בסוק שדות
של אלול.

דבר ספר נחמד ונחוץ סיפורים אמת״ם
המעוררת את האדם לעבדו ה׳ ויראתו
על הקדושים והחסידים לחיזוק באמונה
ונקיון המדות. ולכן הנני מברכך
שתצליח בפעולך לזכות את הרבים
ויכתב הדברים כדאי אלוי דק.

בידידות ויה״ר
ידידות ואהבה
משה אהרן שטרן

---

22 Yechezkel Street - POB 5036; Jerusalem 91 050; Israel
Tel: (972-2) 823-933 Fax: (972-2) 825-537 Home: (972-2) 664-425

הסכמת הרב יהודה זאב סג"ל זצ"ל

Rabbi J. W. SEGAL
40 Broom Lane, Salford, M7 OFJ
Telephone: 061-792 6343

Principal
Manchester Talmudical College
"Saul Rosenberg House", Seymour Road
Manchester, M8 6BQ Telephone: 061-740 0214

ב"ה

יהודא זאב סג"ל
ראש הישיבה, מנשסתר

אור ליום ו' עש"ק פ' ויקהל תשנ"ב

לתלמידי היקר והחביב ר' יוסף יונה וייס שליט"א

שמחתי במה שרחש לבך להוציא ספר שבו נמצא סיפורים אמיתיים, שמהם יוכל הקורא לקבל התעוררות וחיזוק לתורה לעבודה ולתיקון המדות והנני מברכך שתצליח בזה וזכות זיכוי הרבים יעמוד לך שתתברך ביחד את ב"ב יחי' מד' יתברך בכ"ט ותזכה לבנין רבנן וחתנין רבנן.

אוהבך יהודא זאב סגל

This letter of approbation from the Manchester Rosh Yeshiva zt"l was written with the publication of Visions of Greatness Volume I.

הסכמת הרב נתן וואכטפויגעל שליט"א

בס"ד

נתן וכטפוגל
בית מדרש גבוה
לייקוד נ.ו. דז.

אדר א' תשנ"ב

הרב יוסף יונה ווייס שליט"א הראה לי חיבור המכיל סיפורי מעשיות מאת גדולי התורה והמעש, המעוררים את קוראיהם לאהבתו, יראתו, ועבודתו של הקב"ה ולהתמסרות לקיום מצותיו. ובאשר הרהמ"ח שליט"א מוכר לי לבר אוריין וירי"ש והטיב לעשות בחיבורו למען התועלת הנ"ל נתעוררתי ג"כ למסור להרהמ"ח שליט"א איזה גרגרים מאת הגדולים שזכיתי להסתופף בצילם כדי לצרפם לחיבורו הנכבד.

יה"ר שיתברכו מעשה ידיו של הרהמ"ח שליט"א ממקור הברכה ויהנו רבים לאור חיבורו הנכבד. הכו"ח למען זיכוי הרבים ולמען כבוד יראי ה' וחושבי שמו.

This letter of approbation from Rav Nosson Wachtfogel, shlita, was written with the publication of Visions of Greatness Volume I.

הסכמת הרב שמואל קמנצקי שליט"א

ישיבה דפילדעלפיא

בס"ד

בס"ד לסדר ויגש אלי אנא נא

לידיד הרב הגאון ר' אברהם ואנגיל לוצ'ינס
שליט"א נר' הגדול להדפיס חלק ב' מספרו
"חזון הגדולה"

אחרי עלעול הלזו להדפסה.
הרבה גם סיפורי הראשונים אשר שלי והן גדולים
וגן דברים שנראה ודרושים כי כל סיפור יש את הנמשל
שלו. וגם במאמרי הצדיקים ופסקי הראה ולקח את הגדת
גם כל אדם עלי דורות וספר הזה והתנהגו ודעת אנו
המפלגים וגדולים לכל חצאן דרכי הד' וצלחה.
יצאת כח להגדיל מצדיקם ולאוצר הדרים ולחוות
דרכתו דקדוש ונורא נגד מאמינהו.

דידיה צעירה
[signature]

Table of Contents

Introduction 17

BOOK ONE: FAITH AND DIVINE PROVIDENCE

Reunited 23
Wrong Number 29
Returning Home 31
Special Delivery 35
History Unfolds 38
Divine Mission 40
Shaky Revelations 42
Returned Bread 49
Of Faith and Prayer 51
Footing the Bill 55
Encounter 58

Growing Pains 61
A Public Sanctification 64
A Dive in the Right Direction 68

BOOK TWO: CARE AND CONCERN

A Scoopful 73
Entrance Exam 78
A Treasured Handshake 82
Sagacious Memories 87
A Place Twice Yielded 92
Computer Match 95
Fatherly Love 97
Mirror Image 100
Bubble Gum 108

BOOK THREE: NOBLE ATTRIBUTES

A Blessed Shidduch 113
A Solid Investment 116
A Holy Nation 119
Revolving Kindness 122
Bakeries and Bar Mitzvas 127
Good Evening 131
The Right Time 133
I Was So Sure... 136
Family Ties 141

BOOK FOUR: TORAH AND MITZVOS

A Priceless Gift 149
Shabbos Radiance 151
Chanukah Miracle 154
The Angel's Shofar 164
Mitzva Connection 166
Sagacious Attire 174
Guiding Light 176
Holy Counsel 183
The Right Choice 186
A Close Cut 189
Of Bagels and Locks 192
Not for Nothing 194
The Father He Never Knew 196

Glossary ....

Index ....

Introduction

The *gemara* relates (*Nedarim* 66b):

A man from Babylonia went to Eretz Yisroel and married a woman there. Since they were from two different countries, they had some trouble communicating.

Once, the husband told her in his own language to cook two animal's feet. Since she didn't understand his native tongue, she instead made him two lentils. The next day, he asked her for two melons. Again, she misunderstood, and brought him two candles. Frustrated, he snapped at her, "Go break them on top of the *bava*, the doorway." This time, she thought he meant to break them on Bava ben Buta's head. She obediently went to the place where Bava ben Buta was sitting in judgement, and broke the candles over his head.

Bava said to her, "Why have you done this?"

She replied that she was fulfilling her husband's command.

Bava then told her, "You have fulfilled your husband's

wish. May Hashem bring forth from you two sons like Bava ben Buta."

The late Manchester Rosh Yeshiva, *HaRav* Yehuda Zev Segal, *zt"l*, often remarked: When learning a *Chazal* like this, one must think about what he himself would do if he were ever in such a situation. Through this reflection a person comes to recognize the greatness of the Sages, and how much effort is required on our part to refine our characters if we hope to follow in their ways.

Think for a moment about Bava ben Buta's behavior. How difficult it must have been to stay calm and refrain from lashing out at the woman's conduct! Yet not only did Bava ben Buta retain his composure, he even blessed her for her actions. How was he able to react instantly in this manner?

The *gemara* (*Kesubos* 67b) relates a similar incident: A poor man once lived in Mar Ukva's neighborhood. Every day, Mar Ukva would secretly place four *zuz* under the hinges of the man's door. The poor man wondered who his benefactor was, but he never managed to find out.

One day, the poor man was determined to discover the identity of his benefactor. He waited by the door, and as soon as he heard the door hinges being moved, he opened the door.

Mar Ukva had come with his wife that day. When the two of them heard the man coming toward them, they immediately ran away. The poor man continued to follow them, so Mar Ukva and his wife hid in an oven that had recently been cleared. When Mar Ukva's feet began to burn from the heat of the oven, his wife told him to place his feet on top of hers, since her feet were unaffected. From this incident, the *gemara* teaches, "It is better for a person to be thrown in a furnace than to shame his friend in public."

Said Rav Segal: we are not expected to emulate Mar Ukva and his wife, though certainly we should learn the lesson about the importance of not shaming others. Nevertheless, the question remains: how were Mar Ukva and his wife able to react so quickly?

Our Sages understood well the importance of refined Torah attributes. With continual and conscious effort, they constantly worked on their character traits. In this way, when the moment of trial came, they were able to react appropriately.

Mesilas Yesharim (Chapter 21) has a suggestion for those who wish to acquire a strong love for Hashem. "Also helpful is the reading of righteous acts, for these incidents inspire the mind to take counsel and emulate these worthy deeds." With continuous study and reading on the subject of character refinement, our spiritual growth is guaranteed.

It is my hope and prayer that this third volume of *Visions of Greatness* will inspire its readers to reach greater heights in *avodas Hashem*. May we merit to greet *Moshiach* speedily, in our days.

■ ■ ■

In completing the third volume of *Visions of Greatness*, my thanks and praise to *Hashem Yisborach* is best expressed with the following verse, "We cannot thank you sufficiently, Hashem ... and to bless your name for even one of the thousands ... of favors you performed for our ancestors and for us."

There is no limit in expressing *hakoras hatov* for those who assist us. Thus, I would like to thank the following people:

My appreciation to all the distinguished contributors of this volume's stories. It was an honor and merit to share in their personal encounters and absorb the lessons contained therein.

This volume, as well as the other two, is the product of the gifted pen of its editor, Mrs. E. Langer of Lakewood, N.J. Her skillful editing brings each story to perfection.

My sincere thanks to Rabbi Aaron Goldman. As in the previous books, his proofreading and invaluable comments add his singular touch.

I extend deep appreciation to Rabbi Alexander Zissel Ellinson and his staff at CIS for publishing this third volume, particularly for his constant encouragement and personal care to ensure its professional presentation.

I have the good fortune to serve in such a worthwhile *mosad haTorah* as Mesivta Ohr Chodosh and Bais Medrash Ohr HaTalmud. Headed by its *roshei yeshiva*, Rabbi Binyomin Friedland and Rabbi Yosef Gelbwachs, my respect for them grows as I observe the special care they bestow on each *talmid* who enters their *yeshiva*. A special note of thanks for their constant encouragement.

A note of gratitude to Rabbi Yedidya Einhorn, *menahel* of Torah V'Yirah D'Satmar of Lakewood, for the privilege of allowing me to serve in such a wonderful *mosad haTorah*.

No words are adequate to express my gratitude to my parents, Mr. and Mrs. Eliezer Weiss, my brother Reb Shlomo and my in-laws, Rabbi and Mrs. Chaim Yaakov Davis and family. May they all be blessed with *kol tuv*.

To my wife, Tova, whose unending patience and encouragement sets the tone in our home of love of Hashem and His Torah; and to all my children, for sharing their excitement with me as we shared these stories together. May we merit to raise our children to Torah, *chupah* and *maasim tovim*.

Yosef Y. Weiss
Elul, 5757 (1997)

1

FAITH AND DIVINE PROVIDENCE

Reunited

■ ■ ■

Wrong Number

■ ■ ■

Returning Home

■ ■ ■

Special Delivery

■ ■ ■

History Unfolds

■ ■ ■

Divine Mission

■ ■ ■

Shaky Revelations

■ ■ ■

Returned Bread

■ ■ ■

Of Faith & Prayer

■ ■ ■

Footing the Bill

■ ■ ■

Encounter

■ ■ ■

Growing Pains

■ ■ ■

Public Sanctification

■ ■ ■

A Dive in the Right Direction

1
Faith and Divine Providence

REUNITED

"*Gut voch!*"

Herschel Rosinsky walked in the door one *motzei Shabbos* and greeted his family. "Ready for *havdalah*, everyone?"

Just then, the phone rang. "Hold on just a second," Herschel called, and picked up the phone. "Hello?"

"Hi, *gut voch*, Herschel. Have you looked at your mail yet?"

"Looked at my mail?" Herschel asked his sister in surprise. "I just walked in the door, and I haven't even made *havdalah* yet."

"Well, just check to see if you received a book in the mail over *Shabbos*."

Sure enough, there was a big clear package with Lakewood Cheder School on the return address.

"I have the book," he told his sister. "Is there something

really important about this? Can't I make *havdalah* first?"

"Open the book now," she insisted. "Turn to page thirty-five, and read the story there. You can call me back afterwards."

With that, she hung up.

Herschel was completely taken aback by his sister's strange behavior. What could possibly be in that book? Opening the package, he found that it contained the second volume of *Visions of Greatness*, published by CIS Publishers. He turned to the page his sister had mentioned and began reading about a soldier named Willy Feit, and a boy named Harold whom Willy had befriended.

Herschel read the story in disbelief. The boy's last name had not been mentioned in the book. It turned out that Willy had forgotten Harold's last name, since he had left the military base at Fort Dix, N.J. over thirty years before, but Herschel knew exactly what Harold's last name had been.

It was Rosinsky. And Harold now went by the name of Herschel.

■ ■ ■

Harold had been a young boy then, growing up in Brown Mills, N.J., about five miles from Fort Dix. Harold's father worked in Fort Dix as a civil engineer. While the Rosinsky family was Jewish, Harold's parents were non-religious, and Harold knew little more than the bare fact that he was a Jew.

Harold attended public school. When he was in third grade, his teacher came over to him one morning during recess.

"Why are you here today, Harold?"

"Why shouldn't I be?" the puzzled boy replied.

"Well, today is the Jewish New Year. You're Jewish, aren't you? All Jews should be in the synagogue today."

April 13, 1996

Rabbi Yosef Weiss
c/o CIS Publishers
180 Park Avenue
Lakewood, NJ 08701

RE: Visions of Greatness, Volume II, Page 35

Dear Rabbi Weiss:

I am the Harold that you talked about on page 35. I want to update you about myself, since leaving Fort Dix in 1962-63.

I attended Yeshivas Ner Yisrael in Baltimore, until I graduated high school. I then went to Israel for a year. After my return I worked at Ner Yisrael for a few years and married a Baltimore girl. We now have four children.

Approximately seven years ago, I made a *bar mitzva* for my son. Six months prior to that I wrote to the JWB to try and locate the rabbis and KBs who helped me become *frum*. I wanted the *bar mitzva* to have a dual purpose: #1- the *bar mitzva*, #2- To express my *hakoras hatov* to all the people who were involved in helping me become frum. Only Rabbi Edgar Gross was located, and it was, in fact, our pleasure to have him attend our *simcha*.

It would, likewise, be my privilege to be in touch with you. Please contact me at your convenience.

Thank you,

Herschel Rosinsky

This was news to Harold. When he went home for lunch that day, he mentioned what had happened to his mother.

"Do you think I can go to the synagogue this afternoon, instead of going back to school?"

"I don't see why not," was his mother's surprising response.

That was Harold's first visit to the chapel at Fort Dix. From then on, Harold went to the chapel periodically. In 1963, when his *bar mitzva* drew near, Harold began taking lessons with Rabbi Edgar Gross, the Orthodox chaplain.

One time, as the two were speaking together, Rabbi Gross mentioned that he would really like to get *cholov yisrael* milk on base. Harold had no idea what *cholov yisrael* meant, but he really wanted to help the rabbi out. So he rode his bicycle into the next town, where a dairy farm was located, and walked into the office.

"Do you sell kosher milk?" he asked the secretary.

"Kosher milk?" She looked at him blankly. "What are you talking about?"

"The chaplain on the base would like kosher milk," Harold explained.

"Well, I don't know if we have anything like that," she said doubtfully. "But give me your name and number, and I'll look into it for you. Maybe we can ship it in from somewhere."

Harold left in disappoinment, certain that his attempt had been unsuccessful. But two days later, the secretary was on the phone.

"I have some kosher milk for you. You can come here to pick it up."

Harold went back to the dairy farm and was given a bottle of *cholov yisrael* milk, shipped in from Lakewood, N.J. Harold excitedly rode back to the base and presented the bottle to Rabbi Gross. From then on, *cholov yisrael* milk was available on the base for anyone who wanted it.

As time went on, Harold became a regular at the chapel. He became very friendly with the other KB's (kosher boys). Often, when the KB's were being transported on trucks, they would see Harold walking and wave to him. Harold would wave back and smile.

Rabbi Gross continued to teach Harold his lessons, which were complemented by additional learning sessions with Willy Feit and others on base. Harold's progress was remarkable.

On Friday nights, Harold would come to the chapel before *Shabbos*. After the meal, he would walk back the five miles to his house. In the morning, he would walk five miles both ways, to the chapel and back.

One day, Rabbi Gross abruptly asked Harold if he wanted to go to a *yeshiva*.

"What's that?" Harold wanted to know.

Rabbi Gross thought for a minute. "Well, it's a lot like a military school except that no one carries rifles."

"Sounds good," Harold said eagerly.

It wasn't long before Rabbi Gross took Harold for an interview at Yeshiva Ner Yisrael in Baltimore, where he was accepted.

Life wasn't easy for Harold at first. Harold had a tough time getting the terminology down right. He always found himself calling the *beis medrash* the *beis hamikdash*. Harold was also unfamiliar with the right way to address his *rebbi*. He once walked into a classroom where a lesson was in progress, and the *rebbi* began asking him a series of questions. Recalling Rabbi Gross's description of a *yeshiva* as a military school, Harold stood at attention and answered the questions in the way he thought would be most appropriate: "Yes, sir! No, sir!"

But despite all this, it was only a short time before Harold felt very much at home in the *yeshiva*. He continued to progress in Torah and *yiras shomayim*.

Shortly before *Pesach*, Harold came home for the *yeshiva* intercession. He ran into a problem trying to find somewhere to eat the *yom tov* meals. The best solution would have been for him to eat at the base with the rest of the KB's. The trouble was that since Harold wasn't an officer in the army, he wasn't really allowed to eat there.

The problem was solved when one of the KB's lent Harold his uniform. Harold was only thirteen at the time, but he was tall for his age, and the uniform gave him that extra touch. In this way, Harold was able to have a completely kosher *Pesach*.

Another time when Harold was home from *yeshiva*, he heard about a Jewish man who had developed a nerve disorder and had been placed in the psychiatric ward on base. No civilians were officially allowed to visit him, but somehow the doctor there convinced the authorities to allow Harold to come in. Harold spent a few hours every day learning *masechtas Kiddushin* with the man. After only a short while on this "therapy," the doctors were amazed at the dramatic difference in the man. When Harold had to leave to return to *yeshiva*, the learning sessions stopped, and the man regressed to his original state. Such is the power of Torah!

■ ■ ■

Today, Herschel Rosinsky lives in Baltimore, Maryland with his family. He is an important part of his community and is a former member of the *chevra kadisha*. He sets aside time every day for learning Torah.

After Herschel saw his story in the book, he got in touch

with CIS Publishers, in Lakewood, N.J., who in turn contacted Willy Feit. Harold and Willy were reunited after all those years, and now they and their families share a warm relationship.

WRONG NUMBER

Rabbi Selmar lifted the phone in his North Miami Beach home.

"Rabbi Selmar? Hi, this is Dr. Zvi Chyro[1], from West Kendall. Would you be able to perform the *bris* on my son next week?"

Rabbi Selmar thought quickly. The *bris* would be on *Shavuos*, and it would be too far for him to walk, so he would need to stay at someone's house nearby. Then again, a *bris* often falls out on *Shabbos* or *yom tov*, so it was all a part of his job.

"No problem, Dr. Chyro. But I will need a place to stay in your area."

"Of course, Rabbi Selmar. I'll arrange for you to stay by the *Rav's* house, Rabbi Hershel Becker. He's going to be the *sandek*."

On *Shavuos* morning, Rabbi Selmar walked over to where the *bris* was being held and performed the circumcision. Since the baby had actually been born partially circumcised, there was a small chance of a complication, but he felt confident that all had gone well. Still, he decided to caution

---

[1] *Name is fictitious*

the parents before leaving.

"If you do see anything that worries you, please call me at the *Rav's* home. Let's use a signal, say, ring two times and hang up, and then ring two times again. That way I'll know it's you, and I'll come over right away. I'm sure it won't be necessary, though. Everything seems to be fine."

With that, Rabbi Selmar made his way back to the *Rav's* house for the *yom tov* meal.

That afternoon, the phone began to ring. It rang twice, then stopped. Half a minute later, it rang once, then stopped.

"Maybe that was the Chyro's," the *rebbetzin* said thoughtfully. "I know it wasn't exactly the signal, but it might have gotten messed up. Look, it's a nice day outside. Why not just go over and check it out?"

Rabbi Selmar readily agreed. He grabbed his case and made his way to the Chyro home. Everything seemed quiet. He knocked, but there was no answer.

"Maybe it was a real emergency," he began to worry. "Maybe they went to the hospital!"

Now Rabbi Selmar began to pound on the door, hoping that someone would be able to tell him what was going on.

The door opened suddenly. A surprised family member was groggily blinking at him.

"Why, it's the *mohel*! Is something wrong? What brings you here?"

"I got the phone signal at the *Rav's* house, so I came right over."

"Oh, I'm so sorry. That must have been a wrong number. Everything is fine here! What a shame that you *schlepped* out here for nothing."

"Well, as long as I'm here, let me check on the baby," Rabbi Selmar suggested.

Rabbi Selmar went into the baby's room. The infant

seemed to be sleeping peacefully. He turned the baby over to check on him and immediately noticed that the infant was bleeding heavily. He quickly took action and, with Hashem's help, was able to finally stop the bleeding.

Rabbi Selmar whispered a silent thanks to Hashem for the miracle that had just occurred. If not for those anonymous phone calls, he dreaded to think of what would have happened to the child.

Returning Home

Chaim Hertz[2] was excited about his new job. Fresh out of law school, he had managed to find a position with an old, established firm. Chaim had always enjoyed working with wills, and now he was assigned to this department.

As Chaim thumbed through the files to get acquainted with his new clients, one folder caught his eye. Sheila Ragola was a non–religious Jewish woman who had remained a spinster all her life. Her only family was a nephew, Mark, and a niece, named Cindy, also completely assimilated. As Chaim read through Sheila's will, he was disturbed to find that Sheila had requested that she be cremated upon her death.

From the outset, it seemed that there was little Chaim could do about this. How could he make her understand the importance of a proper burial, as prescribed by Jewish law? Nevertheless, Chaim was determined to try.

Every time Chaim met with Sheila to make changes to her will, he would gently suggest that she reconsider her de-

---

[2] *All names and places are fictitious.*

cision about the cremation. Sheila, however, refused to change her mind.

"Cremation is the cleanest way to go," she said firmly.

"Well, what about Mark and Cindy?" Chaim said, trying another tack. "They won't have a place to visit you."

"What will I need visitors for?" Sheila retorted.

Eventually, Chaim was given Sheila's power of attorney, and he was in charge of looking after her financial affairs and nursing fees during the last years of her life. Over the years, Chaim had become friendly with Mark, Sheila's nephew. Now Chaim tried to persuade Mark to talk to Sheila and ask her to change her mind about the cremation. But Mark was reluctant to get involved.

Chaim refused to give up. He continued to work on Sheila. Every time he visited her, he renewed his plea. And in fact, after some time, it seemed that his tactic was working. Sheila still refused to reconsider, but her refusal lacked the same firmness that it had before. Instead of "absolutely not!", Sheila was responding with "maybe ... but I'm still not sure." Chaim continued to grow more hopeful.

But then Sheila grew senile, and the discussions had to end. Chaim still had not persuaded her to change her mind and it seemed as if he never would.

One day, when Chaim was meeting with Mark about a last supplement to Sheila's will, he decided that he would have to be firm about the issue.

"As an executer who is responsible to deal with Sheila's estate after her passing, I feel that I must make a statement."

"Well, what is it?" Mark asked.

"I hereby state that I will not participate in any cremation because it is not in accordance with Jewish law, and one may not fulfill a wish if it is not in agreement with Jewish law," Chaim said firmly.

Mark was silent for a moment. "You know, I got the impression from my aunt during the last few times that I visited her that she was also moving away from cremation. Maybe we ought to do the burial anyway, even if it wasn't actually changed in the will."

Chaim was delighted at this turn of events. He quickly took the opportunity before it could slip away.

"Let me tell you a little about burial. It actually is a bit more expensive than cremation. But I'll try to keep the extra expense to a minimum."

Chaim called someone he knew who worked in this field and explained the whole situation to him. "Is there anything you can do to help me out here?" he asked.

"I actually have two spots available in an old cemetery on the other side of the city. I think I can accomodate you with this, if you're agreeable to that suggestion."

Chaim discussed the situation with Mark, who agreed to the idea. Without wasting time, Chaim bought the plot and took care of all the necessary paperwork.

Eight months later, Sheila Ragola died at the age of 93. As soon as the nursing home informed Chaim of Sheila's death, he began to make all the arrangements necessary for a proper burial. Mark was contacted, and a small funeral was arranged for the following day. Chaim also got in touch with two rabbis who agreed to deliver eulogies and officiate at the funeral.

The next day, Chaim, Mark and Cindy made their way to the cemetery. Before the funeral began, Chaim turned to Mark.

"Are there any specific points you'd like to mention to the rabbis, before they begin the eulogies?"

Mark thought for a moment. "I'd just like to mention two things. First of all, that my aunt was very fond of her small family, and was always speaking about the earlier generations of her family. And second, that my aunt always spoke about returning to her old roots."

After the eulogies were completed, the small group made their way to the cemetary for the burial. Chaim noticed that there seemed to be almost no room at all in the old, crowded cemetery. They had indeed been very fortunate to have secured one of the last places here for Sheila.

As the burial procession came to the location of the burial plot, Chaim happened to glance at one the monuments right next to where he was standing. He gave a start of surprise. The name on the monument was Ragola! Chaim looked at another nearby monument. That one also said Ragola.

Now Chaim was intrigued. He came closer and made a note of the names on both the monuments. Later, when he had the opportunity, he checked into the names to see who they were.

What he discovered astonished him. The two monuments bore the names of Sheila's grandparents; her grandfather, who had died in 1910, and her grandmother, who had died in 1928. More than that: on her grandfather's monument were inscribed the words, "*Menahel Ho'eida*, leader of the Orthodox congregation. A man who was *osek b'tzorchei tzibur b'emunah*, involved faithfully in the needs of the community."

One of the rabbis commented, "We had said before that she wanted to return to her roots. Now she has indeed returned to her roots!"

Chaim turned to Mark and told him, "I see that this funeral has Divine approval."

SPECIAL DELIVERY

"We are now beginning our descent into the Atlanta airport. Please fasten your seatbelts."

Chaim Finer[3] checked his seatbelt and luggage, then sat back in his seat. The young man had just started a promising job with a telecommunications company, and a large part of his work involved traveling to various parts of the country for sales trips and meetings. Since Chaim had an appointment in Atlanta on Monday morning, he had taken a Sunday afternoon flight. His plan was to stay over in a Holiday Inn for the night so he could get a fresh start on Monday morning.

The plane landed uneventfully, and Chaim made his way over to the motel.

"Here you go, Mr. Finer. Room 11A is just down the hall, on the ground floor."

Chaim settled down and tried to get some sleep. But the longer he tried, the more restless he became. He tossed from side to side, trying to get comfortable, but he just couldn't fall asleep. Finally, out of sheer exhaustion, he managed to doze off.

The ringing of the phone jerked Chaim awake.

"What's going on?" he mumbled, still half asleep. He reached for the phone. "Yes, hello?"

"Mr. Finer?"

"Yes, speaking."

"This is the front desk. A package was just delivered here for you."

---

[3] *Name is fictitious*

"What? No, it must be a mistake. Forget it," Chaim mumbled, hanging up the phone.

Chaim turned over and immediately dozed off. But two minutes later, the phone rang again.

"Mr. Finer, this is the desk again. Please come now to take your package."

Now Chaim was wide awake. And he was annoyed.

"What's going on? I'm not taking any package now. It's the middle of the night!"

Chaim banged the phone down. Sure enough, it rang again.

"Please come get your package now, Mr. Finer."

Chaim sighed. What was the matter with that clerk? Couldn't it have waited until the morning? Well, it was already three o'clock, and he was wide awake. "I may as well go and get the package," he grumbled.

Throwing on some clothes, Chaim stumbled out into the hall and made his way over to the front desk. The entire lobby was deserted at this late hour. The clerk was sitting behind his desk, reading a newspaper.

"Okay, I'm Finer," Chaim snapped. "Where's this important package?"

The clerk looked up, startled.

"Excuse me, sir? Was there something you wanted?"

"Yes, the package!" Chaim said impatiently. "You've been calling and telling me about the package, and I came to get it."

The clerk looked bewildered. "I don't know what you're talking about, sir. I don't know about any package here for you, and I certainly haven't been calling anyone."

Now it was Chaim's turn to look puzzled. Had he dreamed the whole thing? But it had felt so real. And he certainly wasn't walking in his sleep now! No, he definitely had talked to someone on the phone. Who could have called him in the middle of the night?

A sudden loud crash down the hall made both men jump. Scores of screaming people began running out of their rooms.

"What's going on?" Chaim yelled. He and the clerk joined the crowd, pushing their way down the hallway to see what was happening.

Chaim finally broke through the crowd. He was standing at the door to his room or rather, at what used to be his room. Now, two of the walls were barely standing, while a third wall had been demolished completely. And there was a wreckage of metal and machinery strewn across the floor, plowing into Chaim's bed, right where he had been sleeping just a few minutes earlier.

Slowly, the story came out. A guest at the hotel had spent the night drinking more than what was good for him. Coming home in a highly intoxicated state, the man had lost control of his car, which had crashed through the wall of the motel, straight into Chaim's bedroom.

Chaim simply couldn't believe it. He whispered a silent thanks to Hashem for the tremendous *hashgacha* he had just experienced. And Chaim wasn't the only one who understood what had happened. As he raised his eyes, Chaim noticed that the clerk, too, was overcome by what had just transpired. He was staring at Chaim, a look of awe on his face.

When Chaim returned home and related the story to his former *rosh yeshiva*, his *rosh yeshiva* remarked, "I'm not enough of a *chassid* to tell you that you had a revelation of Eliyohu Hanavi. But ..."

History Unfolds

Rabbi Chaim Charnas still has fond memories of his early days in Monsey, New York, when he learned in Beis Medrash Elyon. It was the early 1950's then, and Monsey in those years was host to a tiny Jewish populace.

R' Rafael Eisenberg was one of the early pioneers who helped tranform Monsey into the vibrant Torah community it is today. R' Rafael was also very active in outreach, and dedicated his life to bringing others close to Torah.

Shortly before *mincha* one *Shabbos* afternoon, Rabbi Charnas noticed R' Rafael entering the *beis medrash*. Standing at his side was a tall United States Army officer, a three–star general who was dressed in complete army uniform.

R' Rafael's guest was General Lee Thompson[4]. The general had come to visit R' Rafael to acquire a book about faith that R' Rafael had recently written, called *The East–West Conflict*. He ended up taking one copy for himself and another for his good friend, General Dwight D. Eisenhower.

The general was known for his belief in G–d, His Torah, and His people Israel. He also believed that everything that G–d does in this world is for the sake of Israel, and that the whole world is dependent on their repentance. Several times, the newspapers had reported that, on a number of occasions, the general had gone over to Jews and had admonished them to repent and help make the world a better place. Rabbi Shlomo Breslauer, a *rebbe* in Yeshiva Spring Valley, recalled that the general had once spoken to the children in the school. While pointing to the *aron kodesh*, he had said, "Children, I

---

[4] *Name is fictitious*

have been over the whole world, and I have been through much over the years. I have come to the conclusion that the only worthwhile thing in this world is your Torah."[5] Rabbi Herschel Mishinsky, another *rebbe* in the same school, mentioned that the general had shown the children a rock he had acquired in Israel which bore the image of the *sneh*, the burning bush, and had described his emotional reaction when he had flown over the Sinai desert.

Curious, Rabbi Charnas decided to walk back from *shul* together with R' Rafael and his unusual guest. As they made their way home, Rabbi Charnas heard the general telling R' Rafael a remarkable story.

"You know, I was second-in-command in the Air Force in the Pacific during World War II, after the Japanese attack on Pearl Harbor. Later during the war, we had orders to bomb Shanghai. We had excellent intelligence sources from that area[6], and I knew that the Mirrer Yeshiva, as well as thousands of other refugees, were interred in the ghetto and the area around it. I personally made sure that no bombs were ever dropped on the areas where the Jews were located[7]."

Rabbi Charnas listened in amazement to the general's story. Imagine! he thought to himself. None of the Jews in Shanghai had been aware of the danger they were in. This

---

[5] *As told by Rabbi Shlomo Breslaur, Rav of Cong. Beth Tefilah in Monsey*
[6] *This point has been researched and confirmed.*
[7] *R' Rafael mentioned to the general one incident when a shell had hit a house where a Jew was living in the basement, and the Jew was killed. The general was dismayed, and he asked R' Rafael where the house was located. When R' Rafael described the house's location, the general replied that he knew about that bombing; the house had been targeted because it was occupied by enemies. He had not been aware that a Jew had been living in the basement.*

general had served as Hashem's tool in saving their lives.[8] "Your miracles that are with us every day, and for your wonders and favors in every season, evening, morning and afternoon." (*Modim* prayer)

POSTSCRIPT:

In 1965, R' Rafael Eisenberg and his wife settled in Israel. Mrs. Eisenberg recalls that one afternoon, her neighbor came running into her house, describing the interview she had just heard on the radio. The person being interviewed was a United States general who had been in charge of the bombings in Shanghai. Now, he was in the process of undergoing a Jewish conversion[9]. And he thanked the Eisenberg family for their inspiration.

DIVINE MISSION

The following story was related by Mr. Daniel Diena of Toronto, Canada.

They had already consulted with Torah leaders. Now they were ready to begin. Filled with a sense of purpose, several members of the Toronto community were about to start

---

[8] *According to Dr. David Kranzler, an authority on the Shanghai refugees, the facts are plausible, and the general's claims seem to be well-founded. They are also consistent with the intercessions made by R' Avrohom Kalmanowitz with the U.S. Government, on behalf of the Mirrer Yeshiva and the other refugees in Shanghai.*

[9] *Actual conversion has not yet been confirmed.*

constructing the *eruv* around the entire city.

After doing a lot of research, the group discovered that in many places, the railroad tracks around the city were not enclosed by fences. This was absolutely necessary for the construction of the *eruv*. To remedy the situation, members of the *eruv* commitee called the local train company to enlist their help in fixing this problem.

It took a lot of time and effort, but the train company finally agreed to allow the repairs. They also promised a large amount of money for funding the project.

The amount of work was staggering. Over 32 linear miles had to be covered by foot, and notes had to be made of exactly where repairs were necessary. Fortunately for the *eruv* committee, they were not completely on their own. The train company appointed a senior manager to help oversee the necessary repairs.

Joe Achtman was a non–observant Jew, and his dedication to the *eruv* project was incredible. He did everything he could to ensure the project's success.

Joe also had the right connections. "You need a contractor to fix the fences? No problem!" The owner of the largest fence company also happened to be in charge of the Toronto car racing scene. The man had needed a place to store the concrete barriers used in racing, and he had asked the train company for their help. Now Joe called on him to return the favor.

Joe spent a few times a week walking with the group in their inspection of the fences, and helping them record any problems. The other members were amazed at his dedication to the job. Finally, one Friday afternoon, Joe disclosed his secret.

"My grandfather, who was born in Kelm, was a very religious Jew," he told them. "Recently, he came to me in a dream. He told me that the reason I was put on this world was to help you build this *eruv*.

"After I heard that, I decided to do it right. So I'm doing everything I can to make sure this *eruv* is constructed correctly."

And indeed, looking back, the *eruv* committee was certain that without Joe's help, there was no way the *eruv* would have become a reality.

A week after the *eruv* was complete, the group gave Joe a final call to thank him once again for making the *eruv* possible. A woman answered the phone, and they asked to speak to Joe.

"This is his wife," she said in a trembling voice. "You ... you can't speak to Joe."

"Is anything wrong?" the group member on the phone asked in alarm.

Her voice choked up. Finally, she said, "Joe had a heart attack a few days ago. He was only in his early fifties and now he's gone."

Joe had returned his soul to his Maker with his mission accomplished.

SHAKY REVELATIONS

In January of 1995, Rabbi Meir Jacobovits was on his way to Kobe, Japan for a business trip. His itinerary took him to Hong Kong, Tokyo, Osaka and Kobe. R' Jacobovits had actually been in Kobe only three months before, when an earthquake had shaken the northern part of the country. While he hadn't been affected then, his family continued to have some concern for his safety. It didn't help that his trip was plagued by delays and extensive searches because of local terrorist threats. R' Jacobovits arrived in Kobe in an uneasy frame of mind.

The sights in the street did little to reassure him. It was the last evening of a Japanese holiday, and many young people had clearly been out celebrating. Lines of taxis were busily carrying intoxicated young men back to their homes.

"So much for taking a breath of fresh air," R' Jacobovits sighed to himself. He returned to his hotel room and went to sleep.

In the early hours of the morning, Mr. Jacobovits was greeted to a rude awakening. His bed began moving and shaking from side to side. The building was actually moving about a foot in either direction. Plaster boards fell from the wall and ceiling, and the headboard on his bed collapsed, missing him by mere inches. The room was filled with the sound of breaking glass and crashing walls.

"*Shema Yisrael ... !*" he screamed. He had no idea if he would make it through the next few minutes alive.

The shaking continued for exactly twenty seconds. Finally, the quaking stopped. His bed was now in the middle of the room, instead of against the wall where it had originally been. R' Jacobovits glanced at his watch. It was ten to six in the morning. The rest of the room was in shambles. The only thing that had stayed right where he had placed it was his *tallis* and *tefillin*, which had sedately remained on the window sill.

What should I do now? R' Jacobovits thought frantically. Call my family to let them know I'm all right. But first, I'd better get out of this hotel. Who knows? It might collapse at any moment.

R' Jacobovits quickly got his things together, putting on

his raincoat and scarf. Just then, the emergency lights came on in the room, and a loud announcement in Japanese came out of the speaker.

With a start, R' Jacobovits remembered the *halacha* which states that in case of fire on *Shabbos*, one is allowed to take food with him. "Food!" he said aloud. "I'd better take along something to eat." The bed was jammed up against the small refrigerator in his room, but he managed to shove it away and pull some food out.

"My medicine!" he suddenly realized. "It's lost in all this mess. What will I do?"

R' Jacobovits had a heart condition, and he needed to take his medicine every day. His medicine case simply had to be found. Where to begin?

Then a thought struck him. The night before, he had been looking through his medicine, and for some reason, he had decided to put some away in his suitcase. R' Jacobovits quickly checked his case. Sure enough, half his supply of medicine was in there. With a sigh of relief, he grabbed his suitcase, *tallis* and *tefillin*, and left the room.

The emergency lights were on in the hotel corridor, and a loudspeaker was blaring in Japanese. R' Jacobovits went to the nearest staircase, but found it locked.

"Over here!" a voice shouted.

R' Jacobovits glanced across the hall, where a fellow guest was beckoning to him. "Try this staircase. There must be something wrong with that one."

R' Jacobovits crossed the hallway and started to make his way down six flights of steps. The water pipes had burst, and water was flooding the hall and staircase. Walking carefully, R' Jacobovits managed to carry his suitcase to the lobby.

People were milling around the room, looking dazed. R' Jacobovits spotted a bank of phones and decided to call his office. He remembered how concerned his family had been back in October, and he wanted to allay their fears. "It probably won't go through," he reasoned, "but I may as well give it a try."

Incredibly enough, the call went through. "Do me a favor and call my family," he told them. "Let them know that there was an earthquake in Kobe, but I'm all right. I'll try to keep in touch."

After *davening Shacharis*, R' Jacobovits stepped outside to check on the damage. Broken glass was everywhere. Collapsed buildings and piles of rubble lined the streets. Clouds of black smoke rose above the city, signalling that many fires were burning and that there was no water to quench the flames. Screams and cries for help indicated people were stuck under the rubble.

R' Jacobovits was dismayed by the harrowing sight. But imagine, he mused, if the earthquake had struck just ten minutes later, during rush hour. The death toll and damage would have been that much greater.

R' Jacobovits went back into the hotel and walked over to the front desk.

"Would you be able to get me a taxi?" he asked.

The harried clerk looked at him in astonishment. "A taxi? I don't think that's possible. Look at the streets! How is a taxi going to get through all that rubble? Besides, all the taxis were out late last night. It's almost impossible to get a taxi the morning after the holiday."

"Please try," R' Jacobovits persisted.

The clerk doubtfully walked outside and began to hail a taxi. His expression changed from skepticism to surprise when a taxi pulled over. R' Jacobovits got in and asked the driver to take him to Osaka airport.

"No problem," the man said cheerfully.

Progress was slow through the shattered streets. Looking out the window, R' Jacobovits was astonished to recognize another Jew, Mr. Anav, who was a resident of Kobe.[10]

He tapped the driver on the shoulder. "Could you pull over and let him in?"

The taxi driver obligingly picked up the additional passenger, then continued on his way to Osaka. But before long, he came to a stop.

"What's going on? Why did you stop?"

"Look." The driver pointed to the road ahead. "The pavement has buckled completely. Not only that, but the telephone poles have fallen into the street. We can't get by."

Another taxi passed by just then, going the opposite direction. The driver of that taxi rolled down his window.

"Forget about going to Osaka," he called. "The roads are simply impassable."

"I have an idea," Mr. Anav said. "I know the owner of a certain hotel which is still standing. Why don't we try there?"

R' Jacobovits entered the hotel, hoping to find a room. "We're sorry," he was told, "but there is no water or electricity in the rooms, so you can't stay there. You're welcome to stay in the lobby, though."

"Okay," he sighed, "I guess I don't have any choice." Ideally, he was still hoping to find a way to get out of Japan. But after wandering the streets for a few hours, R' Jacobovits was forced to come back to the hotel. There didn't seem to be any way out.

R' Jacobovits tried his luck with the phones again. But this time, the lines were dead. Worried now about the concern his family would be feeling, R' Jacobovits tried to settle

---

[10] *Mr. Anav's apartment building was built on the same place where the Mir Yeshiva was located during their stay in Kobe.*

down in the hotel lobby. But tremors from the aftershock of the earthquake kept him from dozing off.

When morning came, R' Jacobovits managed to find a trickle of water to wash his hands. He *davened*, then made his way out of the hotel to search for another place to stay. One hotel did have water and electricity, but all the rooms were taken. And so the search continued.

Unexpectedly, R' Jacobovits happened upon one of his business suppliers.

"Listen, I've got a lot of people staying at my house," the man told him. "There's running water and heat. Why not come over and thaw out a little?"

R' Jacobovits was tempted. But it was Wednesday afternoon, and he really wanted to find a way to get out of the country. Since there is a *halachic* conflict about the location of the international dateline, he had made a point of never remaining in Kobe over *Shabbos*. And so, thanking his friend for the offer, he continued on his way.

First: back to his original hotel, to retrieve the rest of his belongings. R' Jacobovits carefully gathered his things together and packed them into his suitcase. Next: find a way out of Kobe. The roads were impassable; no taxis were running. The nearest way to get to Osaka was a train from Nishi–nomiya, a town which, he was told, was ten miles away. So R' Jacobovits buttoned up his coat, tightened his scarf, wrote down the directions and started on his way.

As R' Jacobovits walked along, he was joined for a few miles by a Japanese man who knew a bit of English. The two of them often encountered detours where the directions were written in Japanese. Thanks to his companion, R' Jacobovits was able to continue in the right direction.

After the man left, R' Jacobovits continued walking on his own. He squinted at his watch, then at the signposts he was passing. With a sinking heart, he realized that he had walked for ten miles already and that Nishi–nomiya was still ten more miles away. Clearly, the information he had been given was inaccurate. But there was nothing he could do except continue on.

The sun had set. Slowly, the light faded, until R' Jacobovits was walking in complete darkness. Abruptly, a white blob bobbing along behind him materialized into a small Japanese lady carrying a white shopping bag. She too was going to Nishi–nomiya, and she even spoke a little English. Her white bag helped reflect what little light there was, and R' Jacobovits found that he was able to follow her easily.

But her pace began to pick up. "I'm tired, I'm thirsty, and I'm rushiing," she told him. To his dismay, R' Jacobovits realized that he was falling behind. He stopped to take a small drink of water, though he knew that he would lose his guide.

The white bag was no more than a small glimmer of light, far up the road. Then, as he looked into the distance, it began to grow larger. The woman was coming back for him! R' Jacobovits hurried to catch up, and the two of them walked together. Occasionally, the woman would warn him when they approached dangerous spots on the road.

They began to pass buildings on the outskirts of a city. Nishi–nomiya at last! The train station was just ahead. But a jumble of bricks and rubble told the dismayed travelers that no trains would be running from that station.

R' Jacobovits refused to despair. Putting his trust in Hashem, he pushed on to the next train station. The station was standing. But hope was again dashed when they discovered that the rails had been destroyed.

There was still one more chance. Walking for another mile and a half, R' Jacobovits made his way to the third railway station. The trains were running normally! He had made it.

It was nine o'clock PM. Suitcase in hand, R' Jacobovits had been walking for five and a half hours. Despite the freezing weather, his heart condition, and the lack of adequate food and drink, he had managed to reach his destination. Throughout the entire ordeal, R' Jacobovits had felt no fear, indeed, he had felt as if Hashem had been holding his hand the entire time.

The train arrived, and the travelers boarded. When they arrived in Osaka, R' Jacobovits thanked the woman, and blessed her for her help. He took a taxi to a hotel, where he finally found a working phone.

"I'm all right!" he told his distraught family. "I'll take a flight home tomorrow."

The next morning, R' Jacobovits awoke expecting some stiffness from his marathon walk the day before. But he found that he felt fine. He boarded his flight and landed safely in the United States, where he was reunited with his family.

And he breathed a prayer of thanks to Hashem. "*Chasdei Hashem, ki lo sumnu, ki lo cholu rachamov.*"

RETURNED BREAD

Shlomo Hamelech writes (Koheles 11:1), "Cast your bread upon the waters, in the multitude of days you will find it." Rashi comments that the verse is understood symbolically to refer to one like Yisro, who told his daughters to invite the stranger, Moshe, for dinner. Yisro thought that Moshe was an Egyptian, and he never expected to see him again. In the end, Moshe became his son–in–law, and the leader of the Jews. Moshe eventually brought Yisro under the wings of the Shechinah.

World War II had finally come to an end. Refugees began to make their way into Vienna, hoping to find a place to stay until they were able to obtain visas to their final destination.

Chaya Rivka Klein and her sister Esther were hoping to make their way to Canada. The sisters had lost all their immediate family, and they wanted to find a place where they could start life anew. But the months dragged on, and the girls resigned themselves to making the best of their situation.

One evening, as Chaya Rivka was preparing supper, a knock came at the door. Shaya, an old family friend, stood at the entrance.

"R' Shaya, come in," Chaya Rivka said. "What can I do for you?"

Shaya sniffed the air appreciatively. "It smells wonderful," he commented.

"Do you need some supper? Please, there's plenty of food here. You're welcome to share with us."

"No, no, I don't need anything. But I do have a friend who is very ill in the hospital. His food rations are scanty, and he really could use a good kosher, home–cooked meal."

"Of course! Give me just one minute."

Without even asking the name of the patient, Chaya Rivka quickly got some food together and gave it to Shaya. Shaya, in turn, hurried off to the hospital, where he gave the package to his friend.

Shaya watched in satisfaction as his friend hungrily ate his meal. The good, warm food was exactly what he needed. Soon he was on his way to a complete recovery.

The months passed slowly. But finally the beaurocratic

red tape wound to an end, and Chaya Rivka and Esther got their visas. The trip to Canada was uneventful, and the two girls quickly found jobs and settled down to work.

More than financial stability, though, Chaya Rivka really wanted to get married and raise a family. Friends introduced her to Gershon Samanovits, another Holocaust survivor. Soon there was a wedding celebration, and the two young people began to set up a new life together.

Several months later Chaya Rivka had a surprise visitor. Shaya had come to Canada, and he naturally wanted to visit the two young women.

"Come in, R' Shaya! Let me introduce you to my husband."

Shaya took one look at Gershon, and he started to laugh.

"No need to introduce us I know Gershon well."

He turned to Chaya Rivka. "Do you remember one night when we were in Vienna, when I asked you to give me food for a friend of mine who was in the hospital?"

"Of course I remember. But what ... "

"Well," and R' Shaya pointed at Gershon, "this is the man you made supper for. And now you are reaping the fruits of your labor!"

Of Faith and Prayer

Max Cohen carefully maneuvered his forklift around the floor of his new warehouse. Max had recently started a new business, and he couldn't afford to hire professionals who knew how to use heavy machinery. Until he became more prosperous, he had to pitch in himself, wherever he could. So he took a crash course in the use of heavy machinery, and he often filled orders on his own.

Now a rush order had come in, and Max was eager to fill it. He brought his forklift into position and carefully began lifting a load. Unfortunately, Max was in a bit of a hurry, and he misjudged the amount the forklift could lift.

Suddenly, disaster! The load proved to be too heavy for the forklift. The machine tipped over, Max fell out, and the heavy load, in falling, smashed into his arm as he lay dazed on the floor.

Fortunately, Max was not alone in his warehouse. Another worker was standing nearby, and he took immediate action. He lifted Max, put him in his car, and drove him to the nearest emergency room.

The doctors checked Max over and discovered that the heavy package had completely severed the main artery in his arm. Normally, no doctor at that hospital had the expertise to deal with a severed artery. But it happened that on that day, the head of the vascular department in the city was teaching in that hospital. The doctors immediately called him in on the case, and he began the surgery needed to repair the damage.

By that time, Mrs. Rochelle Cohen had been called and informed of the accident. She immediately came down to the hospital. It was to be another twelve hours, though, before the surgery was finished and she was able to see her husband.

Max was finally taken into recovery, his arm in a splint. "You'll keep on this splint for two weeks," the specialist explained to Max and his wife. "In two weeks, we'll take a look at the arm. We need to make sure that the site does not become infected. If it does, we'll need to perform the surgery again."

Two weeks passed quickly by. And once again, Max was wheeled into surgery. The doctors had indeed found an infection, and additional surgery was needed.

In this manner, nine months went by. Seven times, the doctors checked to see if the site was becoming infected. And seven times, surgery was again needed. The doctor was becoming frustrated. After the final surgery, he called his patient in for a conference.

"I'd like to amputate the arm completely. Obviously, something isn't healing correctly. If we leave things the way they are, we run the risk of the infection reaching your heart. Under the circumstances, I think you'd do better with an artificial limb."

But Mrs. Cohen was adamant. "Please, don't give up. Please keep trying."

Mrs. Cohen went to two different *rabbonim* and asked their advice on her husband's situation. "Should we consider letting the doctor amputate?" she asked.

But both *rabbonim* offered the same response. "Under no circumstances should you allow the doctor to remove you husband's arm," they said firmly. And they offered their blessings for herhusband's complete recovery.

And so an eighth operation was performed. And once again, the infection returned.

Now Mrs. Cohen's relatives joined with the doctor's protestations. "Let the doctor amputate already," they pleaded. "How long can he go on like this?"

The doctor gave her an ultimatum. "I'm only going to try one more time. If the infection comes back after that, you must allow me to remove the arm. There is only so much the arm can take, and I really think we've reached the limit."

Mrs. Cohen was devastated. People were turning on her on all sides. Only her complete faith in Hashem and the words of the *rabbonim* kept her from giving in.

The ninth operation was scheduled. That morning, Mrs. Cohen took only her daughter with her to the hospital.

"Don't speak to anyone," she instructed her daughter. "We're going to spend the entire morning saying *Tehillim*, without any interruptions.

"I once heard the following parable. If a child calls up his mother and tells her that he has no way to get home, she will come to pick him up. But if he tells her that there are a few people around, and that he will try to get a ride with them, she isn't in a hurry to go pick him up as she knows someone else may take care of it.

"In the same way, if we rely on others to help us, then our fate is in their hands. But if we completely depend on Hashem, He Himself will come to our aid."

The operation was scheduled to begin. Just before he went in to surgery, the doctor went over to Mrs. Cohen.

"Remember, this is the last chance. After this, I will remove the arm."

Mrs. Cohen nodded silently. She and her daughter entered the waiting room. They opened their *Tehillims* and began to pray. Silent tears streamed down their cheeks as they prayed for the health of their husband and father.

"Don't be scared," Mrs. Cohen encouraged her daughter from time to time. "Daddy will be fine. Just do your part. Keep *davening* without a stop."

The room was full of people who were sitting and waiting for family members who were in surgery. As Mrs. Cohen sat saying *Tehillim*, she saw a flicker of movement out of the corner of her eye. She and her daughter lifted their heads in time to see a man walk into the waiting room with an arm amputated in the same location where Max was having surgery at that very instant. The man walked aimlessly around the room for a few minutes, then turned and left.

Mrs. Cohen and her daughter looked at each other. Her daughter began to cry.

"Stop," Mrs. Cohen said immediately. "I just know that was the *yetzer hora*. Don't stop saying *Tehillim*. Keep praying!"

As the surgery continued, the same man kept wandering in and out of the waiting room. But this time the Cohens ignored him. They just kept up their *davening*, and kept on saying *Tehillim*.

After a long time, the doctor finally came out of the operating room. "I tried something different this time," he told them tiredly. "I took out all the screws and equipment we had put in at the very beginning, during the first operation. Maybe that was causing the infection. I don't really know. All we can do is wait and see."

Six weeks went by. Six weeks of hoping and praying. Finally, the doctor did another examination. Shaking his head, he turned to Mrs. Cohen.

"I don't know how you managed it, but it worked! The infection hasn't returned. It looks like your husband will be fine."

FOOTING THE BILL

Dr. Aharon Lancz wasn't too surprised when his beeper went off. As a podiatrist, he was used to having sudden emergencies, and he was always quick to respond. Dr. Lancz quickly called his answering service for more details. But this time, he was unprepared for the message he received.

"Dr. Lancz, the Police Department just called here for

you," his receptionist said. "They were pretty nasty on the phone, and they want you to call them back immediately."

Frightened and puzzled, Dr. Lancz reached for the phone and dialed the precinct house. He was connected to a tough-sounding police sergeant, who told him that he was under arrest. He was further informed that if he didn't turn himself in right away, a squad car would be sent to pick him up.

Dr. Lancz stared at the phone in shock. "B-but, Sergeant, I don't understand. There must be some mistake! What could I have possibly done that would warrant this?"

"Sir, we sent you a summons, regarding two hundred dollars which you owe. You chose to ignore it, and now you're under arrest. Will you come down to the station yourself, or will it be necessary for us to pick you up?"

Wishing to avoid an embarrassing scene, Dr. Lancz opted to turn himself in. He grabbed his hat and jacket and quickly made his way to the police station.

Upon his arrival at the precinct house, Dr. Lancz was directed to the office of the sergeant who was processing his case. If the sergeant was surprised to see that Dr. Lancz, the podiatrist, looked the picture of an Orthodox rabbi, he didn't let on.

He asked Dr. Lancz to be seated and began questioning him regarding the summons. Suddenly, the sergeant rose from his seat and closed the door to his office. He drew closer to Dr. Lancz until he stood right in front of him.

Dr. Lancz broke out in a cold sweat. He didn't know what the sergeant could possibly want from him, but he didn't have to wait long to find out.

"Doctor, can I show you my foot?" the sergeant asked.

Taken aback, Dr. Lancz nodded cautiously. The sergeant took off his shoe and sock, and placed his foot on Dr. Lancz's lap.

"I recently had surgery on this foot, and now I can barely put any weight on it. Walking is pure agony for me. Maybe you can do a *mitzva* and help me?"

Dr. Lancz relaxed somewhat. No longer did the police sergeant seem so intimidating.

"Sure, I'd love to help you out," he said. "Why don't we go over to my office, where I can check your foot out properly? Also, I came here in such a hurry, I forgot to bring money with me. I can give you a business check at my office."

The police sergeant readily agreed. But he told Dr. Lancz that they would have to go in a police car, since he was still under arrest until the money was actually paid.

Once at the office, Dr. Lancz examined the sergeant's foot. Some damage had been caused by the surgery. To correct the resulting imbalance, he built the sergeant a custom arch support.

The sergeant placed the arch in his shoe and cautiously placed his weight on it. A smile of relief broke over his face.

"Thank you, doctor! This is much better!"

"Glad to be of service," Dr. Lancz said with a smile.

With the sergeant's foot taken care of, Dr. Lancz now wrote out a check for two hundred dollars, and handed it over to the police officer. The sergeant took the check from him, then reached into his wallet.

"Thanks for the check, doctor. And this is for you."

He took out his insurance card and handed it to Dr. Lancz. After processing the paperwork, the sergeant took the card back, thanked the doctor, and made his way to the door.

The sergeant was on his way out when he paused. "Dr. Lancz, before I leave, I must tell you something really interesting. You know Rosh Hashana was just a few days ago. My foot was bothering me so much that I was simply unable to walk. So I drove to the synagogue.

"When I got there, I turned my face towards heaven and I began speaking to G-d. 'Every year, I ask that my family have good health, a good livelihood, and lots of success. This year, I'm asking you for only one thing. I'm in so much pain from my foot, all I want is to be able to walk normally again.'

"Today, I decided to go to the synagogue again. Once again, I entreated the heavens, 'G-d, I know you're very busy. Can't you just make a little time to take care of my foot? I promise you that if you make my foot better, I will walk to the synagogue on any day it is forbidden to drive.'

"Dr. Lancz, when you walked into my office today, I knew that you were sent by G-d as a messenger for me. I knew that my prayers had been answered."

Dr. Lancz was deeply moved by the sergeant's tale. As the police officer left his office, he mused to himself, "We say in davening, 'Hashem is close to all who call upon him, to all who call upon him sincerely.' If Hashem answered the sincere prayers of an irreligious Jew, how much more so would he answer the prayers of those who heed his Torah! 'Hashem will do the will of those who fear him; and their cry he will hear, and save them.'" (*Ashrei* prayer)

And by the way, the insurance payment that Dr. Lancz received was just about two hundred dollars, the same amount that he had paid the sergeant.

ENCOUNTER

The following story was related by Rav Moshe Aaron Stern, shlita, Mashgiach of Yeshivas Kaminetz in

Yerushalayim, who heard it from his uncle, R' Nochum Dovid Herman, z"l.[11]

It was a fine spring day in the late 1950's when R' Nochum Dovid entered a suit store in Yerushalayim. He was browsing through the racks when he noticed a colonel in the Israeli army walk in the door.

"Hey, what happened to you?" R' Nochum Dovid heard the store owner say. Startled, he turned to see the owner addressing the army officer. It was then that R' Nochum Dovid noticed that the colonel was wearing a *kipah*.

"Did you fall on your head or something?" the store owner went on. "Since when do you wear a *kipah*?"

The colonel gave the store owner a dignified look. "I have become a *baal teshuva*."

"Really? But you were so anti–religious! What could have happened to make you change your mind?"

"Listen," the colonel said. "I'll tell you my story.

"A few months ago, I was sent to lead a fleet of fifteen tanks in the Sinai into Egyptian territory.

"My men were seasoned soldiers, and fully trained. We knew how to travel through the desert, and our mission was proceeding exactly as planned.

"And then, out of nowhere, I spotted sixty Egyptian tanks. We were outnumbered! Not just that, but each of their tanks was faster and more powerful than any one of ours.

"I could see no way out for us. This was it! It would only be a matter of minutes before they spotted us and attacked.

"I called the men together. 'I'm afraid this is the end for

---

[11] *Son of the renowned, R' Yaakov Yosef Herman, zt"l.*

us. Everyone is on his own now. I'm sorry to let you down, but there's nothing I can do to help us.'

"'Are you giving up?' a voice called.

"Startled, I turned to see who was speaking. A *chassid* with *payot* and *tzitzit* had stood up in the middle of the group.

"'Listen, if you're giving up, then permit me to take charge.'

"I couldn't believe what I was hearing. I also couldn't understand his confident attitude. What did he see that I was missing? There was no way out of our situation.

"Still, I was impressed by his confidence. And after all, what did we have to lose? So I put it to the others.

"'Should we let him take charge?'

"'Sure, why not?' they agreed.

"'Here's your instructions, then,' the *chassid* told us. 'We will go full force ahead. When I give the signal, everyone will scream with all his might and concentration, *'Shema Yisrael, Hashem Elokeinu, Hashem Echad!'* Then shoot your first round of ammunition.

"'With the help of the *Ribbono Shel Olam*, we will survive.'

"Everyone got into position, and the tanks started moving. The *chassid* gave the signal, and everyone screamed, *'Shema Yisrael!'*, following it with a round of fire.

"When the smoke cleared, we saw an amazing sight. All sixty Egyptian tanks had stopped where they were, and the leader had raised the white flag.

"I couldn't figure out what had happened, but I didn't want to lose the opportunity. I quickly took back command of the unit and I announced in Arabic that all the Egyptians should leave their tanks with their hands up.

"The men all walked out of their tanks and began to come towards us. Their commander was leading, still holding the white flag.

"'You see!' I said triumphantly to the commander, when he came close enough. 'We are more powerful than you!'

"'Don't be ridiculous,' he snapped. 'How can you be more powerful? We have sixty tanks, and you have only fifteen. We caught sight of you in the distance, and we came here just to finish you off.'

"'So, why didn't you?' I wanted to know.

"The Egyptian commander glanced up at the sky. 'We saw those twenty airplanes flying above us. There was no way we could have withstood them. They would have destroyed us completely! So we gave up.'"

The colonel looked steadily at the store owner. "I looked up in the sky, and I didn't see any airplanes. Later on, I checked with the army. There hadn't been any airplanes in that area at the time. *Hakodosh Baruch Hu* had shown them those planes to save our lives.

"I have seen the hand of Hashem with my own eyes. How could I not believe in Hashem and not follow in His ways?"

Growing Pains

R' Shlomo Lazar waited patiently in the line at Kennedy Airport as the passengers began to file onto the plane. He and Reb Gedalya Schorr, Rosh Yeshiva of Yeshivas Torah Vodaas in New York, were on their way to a *chasunah* in Los Angeles, where Reb Gedalya was due to officiate. Though they had come to the airport together, the stewardess had been unable to assign them seats next to each other. So when they boarded the plane, R' Shlomo headed off down the aisle after seeing to it that Reb Gedalya was comfortably seated.

R' Shlomo settled himself in his seat. Directly in front of him was an elderly, grey-haired couple, who were playing cards and drinking cocktails, apparently completely oblivious to the passengers around them. R' Shlomo shrugged and opened up his *sefer*.

A short time later, Reb Gedalya came over to R' Shlomo's seat. R' Shlomo stood up and the two of them spoke in learning for a short time. Then Reb Gedalya turned and went back to his seat.

As R' Shlomo sat down, the old man sitting in front of him turned around.

"Was that Rav Gedalya Schor?" he asked in a European Yiddish.

R' Shlomo was taken by surprise. "Yes, it is," he said. "How did you know?"

The old man winked at him. "I once learned by Reb Gedalya. Of course I know him! Tell me, what is he doing these days?"

"Reb Gedalya is the Rosh Yeshiva," R' Shlomo told him. "He is still learning Torah."

The old man shrugged. "He's still learning, hey? Once I was also so foolish. But I finally saw through that nonsense, and now I'm a successful businessman. I live very comfortably in California. I enjoy all the pleasures of the world, and I'm a very happy man."

The old man shrugged again, then slouched back in his seat and went back to his card game.

When it was time for the meals to be served, the stewardess came over to the elderly couple.

"Here you go, Mr. Teichberg[12]," she announced. "It's your special meal."

---

[12] *Name is fictitious.*

R' Shlomo made a special note of the man's name, then went over to Reb Gedalya's seat. R' Shlomo quietly asked him if he knew who the man was. But while Reb Gedalya said that the name was familiar, he couldn't pinpoint exactly who he was.

The flight eventually came to an end. R' Shlomo disembarked with Reb Gedalya, and the two of them went to the wedding they had flown all this way to attend.

Reb Gedalya was returning to New York the next morning, but R' Shlomo's return ticket was for the following Monday. As the hours passed, however, R' Shlomo decided that it would be better to go back to New York the next night, instead of waiting over the weekend. He went to the airport and waited on standby. If there was enough room on the plane, he would be allowed to board.

Fifteen minutes before flight time, R' Shlomo was told that there were a few empty seats, and he would be able to board. R' Shlomo quickly gathered his belongings and stood in line. The aisle of the plane was very crowded, and since R' Shlomo was one of the last ones to board, he waited patiently for the other passengers to take their seats.

The man standing ahead of him looked slightly familiar. When he turned his head to place his belongings overhead, R' Shlomo finally recognized him.

"Mr. Teichberg!" he exclaimed. "Isn't this interesting? We came to California together, and now we're leaving together! But I don't understand why you're going back to New York so soon. Don't you live in Los Angeles?"

Mr. Teichberg turned to R' Shlomo. There was anguish written on his face.

"What does a man know? Hashem is the one who guides the world. 'A mentch tracht und der abeshter lacht'. A man plans his way and G–d laughs."

R' Shlomo couldn't believe his ears. What could account for this man's change in attitude?

"Why do you say that, Mr. Teichberg?" he asked in bewilderment. "Did anything happen?"

"You might say that," Mr. Teichberg said gloomily. "My wife passed away yesterday. I am now taking the coffin to its final resting place in Israel."

A Public Sanctification

Tulsa, Oklahoma: hardly a bastion of Orthodox Jewish life. But to Sam Goldish, along with a small handful of Orthodox Jews, it was home.

Sam had moved to Tulsa in search of a livelihood. Originally from Marietta, Ohio, Sam had started out working for his uncle in Tulsa. One thing led to another, and soon Sam had a good job working as an engineer for the U.S. Government. He settled down and married.

But despite his isolation from the mainstream Orthodox communities, Sam was committed to keeping a Torah way of life. And he did all he could to pass this commitment on to his children.

Once, Sam needed to sell a boat. He put an ad in the local paper, describing the excellent condition of the vehicle and asking $7500.

The advertisement did not provoke very much interest. Only a small handful of people bothered calling to find out more. Of those who did, just one, a man named Stan, made him an offer. But the amount he offered was much less that the amount Sam had wanted to sell it for.

Sam was in a quandary. Should he take the offer? He really had hoped to make more money on the deal. But there didn't seem to be much interest in his boat. Perhaps he'd be best off taking whatever he could get.

Reluctantly, Sam agreed to Stan's price. "But I have one stipulation," he told him. "I want you to give me a certified check from the bank."

Stan looked a bit uneasy. "Uh, okay. Look, I'll get back to you on it."

But the week went by with no further word from him.

Shabbos afternoon, there was a knock on the door. Mr. Goldish found Stan standing on the doorstep with a big smile on his face.

"Look, I brought you your bank check!"

"Oh, I'm sorry," Sam said, "but today is my Sabbath, and I can't do business now."

"Oh, come on. I don't need you to do anything. Here, I'll just put the check down. I'll take care of removing the boat myself. How's that?"

But Mr. Goldish stood firm. "I'm sorry, but I can't take care of it right now. If you come back tonight, though, we can finish up the deal."

Stan grew angry. "What's the matter with you? I have your check, and you're not willing to accommodate me! Well, forget it then. I won't come back at all!"

With that, he left.

Mr. Goldish refused to let the incident mar his *Shabbos* joy, and he savored the holiness of the rest of the day. *Motzei Shabbos*, the phone rang.

"Hi, I'm calling about the ad for the boat. Is it still available?"

"It sure is. You're welcome to come over and see it."

A short time later, two men had arrived to look at the

boat. After circling the vehicle a few times, they decided they were interested in buying it for the full amount that Mr. Goldish had wanted. They gave him the money, took the boat and left.

"Stan," a family member later said, "spells *Satan*, if you use Hebrew letters to write the name. The *Satan* wanted to test you, to see if you were willing to compromise the holiness of *Shabbos*."

Living in Oklahoma as he did, Sam had his share of strange incidents. Oklahoma is in the heart of the so-called "Bible Belt," and many of the non-Jews there were intimately familiar with the Bible and their religion. Living there as a Jew occasionally caused interesting happenings.

Sam worked for the Defense Department. Out of approximately ninety people in his office, he was the only engineer and the only Jew.

In 1975, the local contractor received a large contract to design and produce U.S. army tank driver trainers for delivery to the Israeli Defense Forces. Because of U.S. State Department and congressional involvement, top Defense Department management wanted to stay informed of the contractor's progress. Special meetings were scheduled every month to review the progress and report on any problem areas.

During one meeting, Sam was huddled around the table, along with a dozen co-workers. As he leaned over the table, the office manager sidled over to him and whispered, "Sam, there's a long white thread hanging down from your belt. Let me remove it for you."

Sam was busy, and he didn't realize what it was. "Okay, thanks," he said absently.

As the man tugged on the "thread," Sam quickly realized that he was actually pulling on his *tzitzis*.

"Sam, what in the world is *this*?" the man exclaimed.

"It's okay, don't worry about," Sam said as quietly as he could. "It's a religious garment. I'll take care of it."

By that time, the entire meeting had become distracted by the exchange. Sam could feel all eyes focussing on him as he tried to discreetly tuck his *tzitzis* back in.

"Okay," he said. "Let's get back to the design changes."

But their interest wasn't to be turned aside so easily. One woman, an industrial specialist named Lorene, spoke up.

"Sam, I heard you say that those threads are part of a religious garment. How does that fit into the Jewish religion?"

"It's a commandment in the Bible," Sam said. "We can discuss it more after the meeting."

No way! Lorene drew herself up and addressed the rest of the assemblage. "My father was a Baptist minister. I was raised in the church. I used to sleep on the church pews. I know the Bible backwards and forwards, and I don't recall ever seeing any commandment to wear that garment. Sam will have to cite chapter and verse to prove it to me."

Sam recognized that there was no malice in Lorene's statement. She simply wanted proof and she wanted it now.

Paul, another specialist, chose that moment to chime in. "I've got a Bible in my desk. Let me get it, and maybe Sam can show us where that commandment is."

In less than a minute, Paul had returned with his Bible, a huge King James edition, and placed it before Sam on the conference table. All eyes were now fixed on Sam, awaiting his next move.

Sam tried to think. He knew the commandment about *tzitzis* was in the *maftir aliyah* of *Parshas Shelach*. Trouble was, the Bible he was holding did not have *parshios*, only chapters and verses. Sam had visions of having to scan page after page of the "Book of Numbers," trying to spot the exact location. But what could he do? There was no way to back out of this unexpected corner.

The room was hushed with anticipation. Sam put his thumb firmly on the edge of the book and opened it.

The first thing he saw was the word "fringes." He felt a sudden wave of exultation.

"Here it is," Sam said, trying to sound nonchalant. "Book of Numbers, chapter 15, verses 37 through 41."

Visibly taken aback, Lorene walked over to the open Bible. Sam pointed to the verses, and she read them aloud for all to hear.

"Well, I guess that's one chapter I missed," she said finally. "But Sam, how in the world were you able to open the Bible to the exact page you wanted?"

"You might call it Divine Providence," Sam replied.

Sam has already passed away from this world. But he left behind a proud *kiddush Hashem* in his own corner of Oklahoma.

A DIVE IN THE RIGHT DIRECTION

In 1972, Ephraim Vashovsky's mother first suggested to his father that the family try to leave Russia.

"No!" Mr. Vashovsky said adamantly. "Here in Russia I have a job and a home. Who knows what the future in a strange country will bring?"

His religion played no part in his decision. At that time, the family knew little more about their religion than the fact that they were Jewish.

Nine year old Ephraim was perfectly happy staying in Russia. Ephraim was completely involved in swimming and diving, and he had a real talent for the sport. Every spare moment was spent in refining his technique and reaching his goal of competing in the Junior Olympics.

The day of the tryouts quickly approached. Many children had registered for the tryouts that would be taking place in his hometown of Kishinev. While the competition was fierce, Ephraim knew that he was good, and that he had a real chance of making it into the Junior Olympics in Moscow.

Ephraim watched the tryouts with a feeling of confidence. He knew, even before the onlookers congratulated him, that his performance had been a good one. And indeed, he was sent to the section of the building where the finalists were to be interviewed.

Ephraim took his seat among the other finalists, feeling ecstatic at his accomplishment. How proud his parents would be! His dream was really coming true. As he waited for his turn to be interviewed, he began daydreaming about winning the Junior Olympics.

The instructor soon came over to him and began asking questions: Name, address, school, nationality . . .

With the word "nationality," an alarm went off in Ephraim's head. How should he answer the question? Should he say that he is Jewish? Though he was only nine years old, Ephraim was wise enough to realize that if he was known to be a Jew, it could cause problems. What difference did it make, anyway? So why not just say that he was Russian?

"I am Russian," Ephraim said finally.

"Fine," the instructor said, making a mark on his chart.

Just then an unbelievable thing happened. All fifty people who were sitting in the circle lifted their hands in unison and pointed a finger at Ephraim.

"He is a Jew!" they declared.

Ephraim turned fifty shades of red. He stood there in

shock and embarrassment. The instructor, who had been so cordial just a moment before, now changed his tone.

"Well, due to certain circumstances, and of course because of shortage of space, I suggest that you try again next year," he said firmly.

Ephraim was dismissed. His dream had come to nothing. With a feeling of despair, he turned and ran from the room. He knew he was good. He was one of the best in the room! But he had nevertheless been turned down because he was a Jew.

Back home, Ephraim poured his heart out to his father. "Why should I bother with this anymore?" he cried. "They reject me only because I am Jewish. How can I possibly accomplish anything here?"

Ephraim's father was shaken. He turned to his wife.

"You were right," he said quietly. "There is no place for us here. We will leave Russia."

Ephraim and his family eventually made their way to America. His parents became committed to *Yiddishkeit*, and now Rabbi Ephraim Vashovsky, a *rebbe* in Sinai Academy, teaches Torah to Russian Jews all because the Russians would not let him forget that he was a Jew.

2

CARE AND CONCERN

A Scoopful

■ ■ ■

Entrance Exam

■ ■ ■

A Treasured Handshake

■ ■ ■

Sagacious Memories

■ ■ ■

A Place Twice Yielded

■ ■ ■

Computer Match

■ ■ ■

Fatherly Love

■ ■ ■

Mirror Image

■ ■ ■

Bubble Gum

2
Care and Concern

A Scoopful

In 1976, Senator Henry "Scoop" Jackson was campaigning for the upcoming Presidential elections. While Senator Jackson was not Jewish, his dedication and respect for the Jewish people were remarkable. He was very active in Jewish organizations and backed many projects that were set up to benefit Israel.

R' Moshe Londinski, who at that time was a rabbi in Seattle, Washington, was a big admirer of Senator Jackson. He helped with fundraising and often spoke to help gain the Senator support in his quest for the Presidency.

One Sunday afternoon in early June, R' Moshe received a phone call from the *gabbai* of the Skulener Rebbe, R' Eliezer Zisha Portugal, *zt"l* (1896–1982).

"I'm calling on behalf of the *rebbe*," the man informed him. "The *rebbe* must see Senator Jackson tomorrow at nine o'clock AM. Can you arrange an appointment?"

"Tomorrow? Well, I don't know, it's not so simple. The Senator is in the middle of his campaign, and he's traveling all over the country. In fact, I don't even know where he is right now! I don't think it will be possible."

The *gabbai* was very insistent. "It's important that the *rebbe* speak to the Senator tomorrow at nine."

R' Moshe heard the urgency in the man's voice. "All right," he said, "I'll see what I can do."

The first step was a call to Stan Golub, one of the Senator's main campaign managers.

"Stan, this is Rabbi Londinski. I have to ask you for a favor. I need to speak to the Senator immediately."

"Look, Rabbi, the Senator is in Arizona now. There's no way to get him on the phone there."

"It's important, Stan. I've never asked you for a favor before, but it's urgent that I speak to him right away."

"I'll do what I can, Rabbi, but I'm not guaranteeing anything."

R' Moshe thanked Stan and put down the phone. It rang three minutes later.

"Scoop here! What seems to be the problem? Stan said it was urgent."

R' Moshe was momentarily at a loss for words. He hadn't dreamed that he would get such a quick response! He quickly pulled himself together.

"I just got a call from a saintly *chassidic* rabbi from New York. He says that he must see you tomorrow morning. He's willing to go wherever you are. Will you be able to see him?"

"Let's see, I'm taking the red–eye back to Washington tonight. My schedule is tight, but I'll fit him in first thing in the morning. I'll make sure the rabbi has enough time to tell me what he needs to say."

R' Moshe thanked the Senator and called the *gabbai* back with the good news. The *gabbai* asked R' Moshe to hold on while he relayed the news to the *rebbe*. There was a short pause, and then the *gabbai* got back on the phone.

"The *rebbe* has one more request. Since the *rebbe* only speaks Yiddish, he would like you to be there as an interpreter."

"Me? The *rebbe* wants me to come? I'm in Seattle! That's over three thousand miles from Washington. I'd have to leave immediately and travel overnight if I wanted to get there in time."

The *gabbai* heard R' Moshe out, but simply repeated, "The *rebbe* wants you to be there!"

"All right," R' Moshe surrendered. "If it's that important, I'll be there."

The next morning found R' Moshe in Senator Jackson's office in Washington, D.C. The Senator was already in his office, busy rearranging his schedule so he would have time to speak with the *rebbe*.

The *rebbe* arrived with his *gabboim*. They met R' Moshe in the outer office, and they entered the inner sanctum together. Senator Jackson's inner office was very impressive, complete with magnificent panelled walls and a rich oak mahogany desk. The Senator was, after all, the head of the U.S. Foreign Relations Committee, and a very powerful man.

The Senator greeted his guests and sat down behind his desk, ready to begin the meeting. But instead of speaking to the Senator, the *rebbe* whispered something to his *gabbai*, who in turn whispered something to R' Moshe.

R' Moshe turned pale. He looked helplessly at Senator Jackson

"What is the problem?" The Senator asked curiously.

"Well, ah . . . " R' Moshe took a deep breath. "It seems that the *rebbe* has not had a chance to say his morning prayers. He needs a place where he can concentrate. Would he be able to use your office for a little while?"

"Of course, no problem!"

The Senator immediately stood up and walked with R' Moshe out of the inner office. The two of them stood in the hall, waiting for the *rebbe* to finish.

Twenty minutes went by. By this time, both men were pacing the hall. R' Moshe didn't know what to say to the Senator. After all, it was his office! Fortunately, the office door opened just then, and the *rebbe* himself beckoned them back inside.

Senator Jackson once again seated himself behind his desk. "Now," he said with a smile. "What can I do for you?"

R' Moshe stood next to the *rebbe*, ready to interpret every word. The *rebbe* opened his mouth to speak. But he said just two short words and then burst into tears.

"What's wrong?" the Senator asked in concern.

"I don't know," R' Moshe said in bewilderment.

The *rebbe* was trying to speak through his tears, but R' Moshe couldn't understand a single word. He stood, waiting for the crying to stop, but the tears continued to pour down the *rebbe's* face.

Senator Jackson beckoned R' Moshe over. "Tell the rabbi that I know what he wants," he said abruptly.

"You do?" R' Moshe said, startled. "How?"

"Just ask the rabbi what he wants me to do about it," the Senator told him.

R' Moshe stared at the Senator for a moment, but then he obediently turned to the *rebbe* and relayed the Senator's statement. The *rebbe* stopped crying.

"I want it stopped immediately," he told R' Moshe.

R' Moshe translated the *rebbe's* statement.

"How does he want me to stop it?" the Senator asked.

Again R' Moshe relayed the question to the *rebbe*.

"The Senator knows which buttons to press," the *rebbe* replied.

The Senator reached for the phone, punched in a number and began to speak. And as R' Moshe listened, the story slowly became clearer to him. It seemed that a few days before, the Romanian government had arrested twenty Jews and falsely accused them of currency speculation. They were imprisoned and due to be executed in a few days. The whole situation was a ploy by the Romanian government to pressure the United States into giving them Most Favored Nation status. The Senator, as the head of the Foreign Relations Committee, was also very involved with Soviet Jewry, and he knew of this action by the Romanian government. He had immediately understood what the *rebbe* had come for.

The Senator was speaking to the Romanian ambassador. "As head of the Foreign Relations Committee, I strongly suggest that you immediately call the Prime Minister. Tell him that if those twenty prisoners are not released within forty-eight hours, I guarantee that Romania will never see a cent of American aid. Hair will grow on the palm of their hands before they ever receive America's Most Favored Nation status."

The Senator put the phone down and looked up at R' Moshe. "Tell the rabbi that it has been taken care of."

The *rebbe* smiled and warmly shook the Senator's hand.

Within forty-eight hours, all twenty prisoners had been released and brought to Eretz Yisrael.

Once again, R' Moshe had seen Senator Jackson's concern for the Jewish people. R' Moshe was curious about this, and one time he took the opportunity to ask the Senator why he cared so much about the Jews.

Senator Jackson smiled. "Three reasons. One, I was a prosecutor during the Nuremberg trials. I saw how much the Jews had suffered in the concentration camps, and I resolved to do whatever I could to help them.

"Two, my mother, a widow, was a housekeeper for a Jewish family in Evret, Washington. They treated her very well. They gave her extra food and money during the Depression years to help her raise her family. In her will, my mother asked that her children should always be good to the Jews.

"And finally, when I was a young boy, there were a few Jews I would always help out on Saturday. They always treated me nicely and gave me tips after their Sabbath was over."

The Jewish people, by practicing their Torah–true *middos*, had instilled a feeling of mutual respect into a man who later rose to a position of power, and was able to reciprocate their kindness.

ENTRANCE EXAM

The day R' Mordechai Susna graduated Yeshivas Yaakov Yosef in 1951 was one of the happiest in his parents' lives. More than anything, they wanted their son to grow up to be a *ben Torah*, and this was one big step in the right direction.

But the Susnas did not want to stop there. Next on the agenda was enrolling R' Mordechai into a *yeshiva* for higher learning. To this end, Mrs. Susna went to visit Rabbi Kalman Avraham Goldberg, the *rav* of Adas Yisroel Shul on the East

Side, who was well known for his enthusiastic support for continued yeshiva learning.

"Your son is young," Rabbi Goldberg told Mrs. Susna, "but I think you should look into Bais Medrash Govoha, in Lakewood. Rav Aharon Kotler is the *rosh yeshiva* there, and your son can do no better than to learn by him."

The Susnas lost no time in contacting Reb Aharon, who promised to be in touch with them sometime in the near future.

One evening shortly afterwards, as Mordechai was on his way to bed, there was a knock at the door. In walked Rabbi Goldberg.

"Guess what, Mordechai! I've arranged an interview with Reb Aharon! He's able to see you right now."

"Now? But–but..."

"Yes, right now! I know it's late, but you can't afford to miss this opportunity."

Mordechai was reluctant. "This is so sudden. I haven't had any time to prepare! How can I speak to the great Reb Aharon Kotler in Torah without spending some time beforehand preparing what I'm going to say?"

"Don't worry," Rabbi Goldberg insisted. "It will be fine. But you must come now!"

Mordechai allowed himself to be persuaded, and the two of them went off to the West Side, where Reb Aharon was staying.

Mordechai stood awkwardly when they came into the room. Reb Aharon beckoned him over to the table, then pushed his hat back on his head and sat down in his chair. Seeing the *rosh yeshiva* so relaxed helped Mordechai calm down, and he felt his tension receding.

As soon as Mordechai was comfortable, Reb Aharon began asking him questions about the *gemara* he was presently learning. Mordechai tried to answer the questions, but as the session went on, he felt his nervousness returning. "Forget it," he though glumly. "I'm not doing well at all."

After a short while, Reb Aharon stopped the questions. Then Rabbi Goldberg, who had been standing at the side of the room the entire time, came forward.

"Do you mind stepping out for a minute, Mordechai?" he asked the young man.

Mordechai obediently stepped out of the room. He heard voices from the other side of the door, but he couldn't make out what they were saying. Gloomily, he paced the small hall, reflecting upon the questions Reb Aharon had asked him, and mentally chastising himself for his poor showing.

Ten minutes later, he was called back into the room. As Mordechai approached the table, a smiling Reb Aharon told him that he had been accepted into the *yeshiva*.

Mordechai couldn't believe his good fortune. He immediately made preparations to travel to Lakewood, and he soon joined the other *talmidim* in Beis Medrash Govoha.

Mordechai soon discovered that he was the youngest *bachur* in the *yeshiva*. He realized what a great opportunity he had been given, and he was determined not to waste a moment. He learned as much as he could, not only from Reb Aharon himself, but also from the other *bachurim*, who were much older and more experienced than he was. (In fact, Mordechai used to stand up for every single *bachur* in the Lakewood Yeshiva!) Considering his youth, Mordechai was hard-put to explain how Reb Aharon had been willing to accept him into the Yeshiva.

The mystery remained for several years, until the conversation Rabbi Goldberg had had with Reb Aharon finally came to light.

Rabbi Goldberg had been describing Mordechai's family to Reb Aharon. He depicted his mother's parents as upright Torah Jews; her father owned a hardware store, and he sat in the store with a *sefer* in his hands, which he learned from in between serving customers.

He then went on to describe Mordechai's father. He told Reb Aharon that the orphaned R' Yonah Susna had come to America from Russia at the tender age of thirteen. The young Yonah had the good fortune to meet a G–d fearing man, who was a *shamash* in a *shul* on the Lower East Side of New York. The man offered to take the young boy into his home. There, he not only cared for the orphan, but he even taught him Torah.

When R' Yonah grew up and married, he and his wife decided to build a home based on Torah and *chessed*. In the *shul* where R' Yonah *davened*, Beis Medrash Hagadol, there were many poor, homeless Jews who slept in the back of the shul, clothed in ripped and tattered garments. Every morning after davening, R' Yonah would bring these people to his home for breakfast, where his wife served them fresh rolls and coffee.

Unfortunately, these impoverished Jews were often infested with lice, and eventually his wife discovered that her home, too, was becoming infested. Regretfully, the Susnas decided that they would have to come up with a different way to provide for these people. Instead of bringing them into her house, R' Yonah's wife sent the rolls and coffee with him to shul every morning.

One morning after *davening*, a poor man came over to R' Yonah.

"Can I ask you for a favor?" he whispered.

"Of course, what can I do for you?"

The man looked around furtively. "I'm in desperate need of a new set of clothing," he told R' Yonah quietly.

R' Yonah's heart was torn. On the one hand, he knew

that he could not bring the man to his home. One the other hand, he desperately wanted to help out this poor Jew.

Suddenly R' Yonah had an idea. "Wait right here!" he told the man.

R' Yonah went into a private room, removed his own clothing, and put on his heavy coat. Then he gave the poor man his clothing and returned home with only his coat.

When Reb Aharon heard this story, he said to Rabbi Goldberg, "A son of such a holy Jew I most definitely want in my *yeshiva!*"

A TREASURED HANDSHAKE

R' Moshe Blau, a Torah leader in Eretz Yisrael, came to Vilna in the 1930's. Rav Chaim Ozer Grodzinski,zt"l, Vav of Vilna and the gadol hador of his era, instructed his attendant to show R' Blau the "treasures of Vilna."

When they returned, Rav Chaim Ozer asked, "So where did you go?"

The attendant replied, "I showed him the Gaon's kloiz, the old cemetery, the Strashun library..."

"That's fine," R' Chaim Ozer interrupted, "but you neglected to take him to see Vilna's living treasure, Rav Avraham Yeshayahu Karelitz."[13]

---

[13] *Later to become the Chazon Ish.*

Yossi[14] slouched on the couch in the living room, staring morosely at the ceiling. Here it was, *chol hamoed Sukkos,* and he had absolutely nothing to do. All his friends had gone on trips, but he was stuck in Williamsburg by himself. What kind of vacation was this, anyway?

He stood up restlessly and wandered into the *succah.* Even the fresh-smelling *schach* and the cheerful decorations couldn't lighten his spirits. What should he do with himself for the next few days?

As he stood there, it occurred to Yossi that his friend Shmuely hadn't gone anywhere, either. Maybe, he thought with rising hope, the two of us could do something together. He hurried back inside the house and quickly dialled his friend's number.

"Hey, Shmuely, how're you doing?"

"Bored," came the sigh over the receiver.

"Maybe we can do something exciting together," Yossi suggested eagerly.

"Yeah?" Shmuely said, sounding a little more interested. "Like what?"

"Well, let's see..." Yossi thought for a moment, then was struck by a blinding idea. "I've got it! Let's go tomorrow morning over to the Lower East Side and *daven* at Mesivta Tiferes Yerushalayim. We can get to see Reb Moshe!"

Rav Moshe Feinstein, *zt"l* (1895–1986), the *gadol hador,* was New York's living treasure. Yossi had never seen him in person before. Now *that* was a *chol hamoed* trip worth taking!

"Hey, that's a good idea," Shmuely exclaimed. "Why wait for tomorrow? Why don't we go now?"

"It's after six already," Yossi pointed out. "We'll have a

---

[14] *Name is fictitious.*

better chance of seeing him if we go tomorrow morning for *shacharis*. What do you say?"

"I'm all for it," Shmuely declared. "I'll meet you at the corner next to your house at 6:30 tomorrow morning."

When Shmuely arrived the next morning, he found Yossi waiting impatiently. "Are you ready? Then let's go!"

The two young teenagers took the subway train to the Lower East Side. Excited and stimulated, they arrived at the *beis medrash* several minutes before *shacharis* was scheduled to begin. Eagerly, they looked around, but Reb Moshe had not yet arrived.

"It's still early yet," Shmuely whispered to Yossi. "I'm sure he'll come in any minute now."

Yossi nodded, his gaze fixed on the door in the back of the *beis medrash*. Today was *chol hamoed*; in addition to the regular *davening*, there was *hallel, krias haTorah, mussaf,* and *hoshanos*. Surely, Reb Moshe would come!

The door opened. The boys' hearts jumped, then settled back into place as a boy their own age came inside. The door opened again, and again, but Reb Moshe still did not arrive. Yossi and Shmuely glanced at each other anxiously. *Davening* would begin in just a minute or two. Where could Reb Moshe possibly be?

The seconds ticked by. The *chazzan* began the *davening*. And Reb Moshe still had not come.

When *shacharis* and *mussaf* were over, Shmuely approached one of Reb Moshe's *talmidim*.

"Excuse me," he said somewhat timidly. "Can you tell me why Reb Moshe was not here this morning?"

Then man sighed. "Reb Moshe has not been well lately," he explained. "He often isn't well enough to come to *shul*."

Shmuely thanked the man, then went back to Yossi and reported. Disappointed, the boys had no choice but to go back to Williamsburg, their mission unaccomplished.

Yossi sat in the *succah* that afternoon, staring blankly at the walls. He was still upset that his wonderful idea for a *chol hamoed* trip hadn't worked out.

As he sat there, his *rebbe's* words suddenly came to mind: "A mature person is not discouraged by disappointments. He perseveres until he achieves his goal."

Yossi sat up straight. True, Reb Moshe hadn't been well enough to come to *shul* that morning. But that didn't mean Yossi couldn't try again tomorrow!

Then he slumped back into his chair. "Oh, what's the use?" he said aloud. "Why go again? Reb Moshe isn't well. He probably won't come again tomorrow, either."

You never know, a tiny voice whispered inside his skull.

Yossi made up his mind. He would try again tomorrow.

At 6:25 the following morning, Yossi crept out of the house and hurried through the chilly air to the subway, where he once again rode to the Lower East Side. As the train clattered down the tracks, Yossi silently begged Hashem to send Reb Moshe a speedy recovery so he would be able to attend the *davening* and Yossi would be *zocheh* to see the *gadol hador*.

In good time, Yossi arrived at Mesivta Tiferes Yerushalayim. With an accelerating heartbeat, he prepared to *daven* and then twisted around in his seat so he could watch the door in the back of the *beis medrash*.

Just as Yossi was about to give up hope, the door opened one last time. Reb Moshe had arrived!

Yossi swallowed hard as he watched the *gadol hador* slowly walk through the *beis medrash* toward his seat. Reb Moshe's noble features and glowing *hadras panim* seared through his brain. Yossi found himself *davening* that morning with an intensity and concentration like never before.

As the *davening* came to a close, Yossi found himself

watching Reb Moshe in his *tallis*. How saintly he looks, Yossi thought with awe. Just like... like... Yossi struggled, but he couldn't come up with an appropriate comparison. It didn't matter, he decided. The important thing would be to give Reb Moshe a *"sholom aleichem"* after *davening* and ask him for a *beracha*.

At the conclusion of *mussaf*, Yossi began to walk towards the front of the *beis medrash*. He had taken only three or four steps when he felt a hand on his shoulder. Turning, he saw the same man whom Shmuely had approached the day before.

"Due to Reb Moshe's ill health, no one is to impose on him, or even give him *'sholom aleichem'*."

Yossi opened his mouth, then shut it. There was nothing he could say. Crestfallen, he stood where he was, watching Reb Moshe as he slowly removed his *tallis*.

At least I merited seeing him, Yossi tried to tell himself. Even if he couldn't greet the *gadol hador* personally, at least he had seen Reb Moshe face to face. That was better than nothing, wasn't it?

No! Yossi's expression firmed. He'd come this far. One way or another, he would persevere. If he couldn't actually speak to Reb Moshe, perhaps there was something else he could do.

At once, an idea flashed into Yossi's mind. He may not be able to wish Reb Moshe *"sholom aleichem,"* but he could serve the *gadol hador*, even in a small way. He turned, pushed his way through the crowd of men watching Reb Moshe, and rushed to the door at the back of the *beis medrash*. At least he could hold the door for Reb Moshe as the *gadol hador* walked out.

From his vantage point at the door, Yossi watched breathlessly as Reb Moshe finished putting away his *tallis*. The crowd parted respectfully as Reb Moshe slowly made his way to the door.

As Reb Moshe approached, his eyes met Yossi's for a moment. Then, disregarding his ill health, he smiled and offered Yossi his hand.

Awestruck, Yossi lifted a trembling hand and grasped Reb Moshe's. The *gadol hador* smiled again, then walked outside and was gone.

Yossi barely needed the subway to get back home to Williamsburg; he was practically floating on air. Not only had he been *zocheh* to see Reb Moshe and serve him in some small way, but he had even been granted the opportunity to shake Reb Moshe's hand in *"sholom aleichem"*! It was a moment that Yossi knew he would treasure for the rest of his life.

SAGACIOUS MEMORIES

Rabbi Eliyahu Roman describes the relationship he formed with the Kopicznitzer Rebbe, Rav Avraham Yehoshua Heschel, zt"l(1887–1963).

The clatter of silverware and the low hum of voices filled the dining room as Eliyahu Roman deftly maneuvered his tray around the crowded tables. On summer break from the Philadelphia Yeshiva, seventeen year old Eliyahu took a job to earn some extra money.

While Eliyahu may have resembled his fellow students in many ways, he was indeed different, if only through his life experiences. Eliyahu, a native of Philadelphia, PA, had lost his father when he was a young teenager. Many children may have given in to their despair. But Eliyahu remained strong, and persisted in his dream of continuing his full time learning and becoming a *ben Torah*.

Now, in the summer, he had hoped merely to earn some money. But because of a very special guest at the American Hotel in Sharon Springs that summer, Eliyahu ended up forging a relationship with a great *tzaddik*, the Kopicznitzer Rebbe, Rav Avraham Yehoshua Heschel.

The Kopicznitzer Rebbe had a heart condition, and he had come to the hotel for three weeks of rest. But "rest" was one word that was not on the Rebbe's agenda! Shortly after he arrived, the Rebbe befriended an 83 year old man who was also a guest at the hotel. The man was not Torah observant, and the Rebbe tried, through his renowned gentleness and warmth, to bring him closer to Torah.

One day, the Rebbe had to return to the city to serve as *sandek* at a *bris*. Before he left, he went over to his new acquaintance.

"You know, it says in the Torah that a man's alloted period is seventy years. Now that you're 83, it's thirteen years past the end of your allotment. That means that you're having your second *bar mitzva*."

"Another *bar mitzva*, hey?" The man liked the idea.

"I'd like to make a *kiddush* in honor of your *bar mitzva*," the Rebbe told him. "But there is one condition. You must accept the *mitzva* of putting on *tefillin* for the rest of your life."

The man thought for a minute. "Okay, I accept that."

On his return from the city, the Rebbe brought back trays of cake, *kugel*, *schnapps*, and a pair of *tefillin*. The following morning, the man put on the new *tefillin* and joined the Rebbe's *minyan*. And the Rebbe made a big *kiddush* for the man's *bar mitzva*.

The man kept his word. Every day, he came to the *minyan*

and put on his *tefillin*. By the end of the summer, he and the Rebbe had formed a strong bond.

■ ■ ■

One *erev Shabbos*, Eliyahu was walking past the Rebbe when he heard him say, "Ah Elya, *du lost men nisht oislaidigin*. Here it isn't possible to empty out the pockets."

Later, someone explained the Rebbe's words. On *erev Shabbos*, the Rebbe used to give out all his money to the poor and the needy. In Sharon Springs, he did not have this opportunity. And so the Rebbe was voicing his distress.

■ ■ ■

The Rebbe had his own food and utensils at the hotel. His family would prepare his meals, and Eliyahu would serve him. Every time Eliyahu gave him his food, the Rebbe would thank him profusely, and then say, "Elya, you are a very fine young man. I hope I don't cause you any trouble."

Once, Eliyahu happened to give the Rebbe a larger portion of food than usual. The Rebbe stopped him. "I don't like to overindulge," he explained. "Could you take some back, please?"

But that didn't stop the Rebbe from giving Eliyahu his usual *beracha*.

■ ■ ■

It was the Rebbe's first Friday night at the hotel. Together with his family and some *chassidim*, he began the Friday night *tisch*. Eliyahu finished serving the rest of the dining room, and now he approached the Rebbe's private room.

"Wait, Elya," the Rebbe called to him. "Don't serve yet. First sit down with me and have something to eat. Drink a *l'chaim*."

Eliyahu sat down, a bit overwhelmed. Taking a little to eat, he sat quietly, enjoying the rest and his proximity to the great *tzaddik*.

After a short time, the Rebbe told him, "Now that you are a part of us, you may, if you wish, begin to serve the meal."

■ ■ ■

During that summer, Rav Avrohom Kalmonovitz, *zt"l*, *rosh yeshiva* of the Mirrer Yeshiva in New York, who had been staying in a different hotel in Sharon Springs, would come every day to visit the Rebbe. Once after Rabbi Kalmonovitz left, the Rebbe commented, "*Der yid shpirt der golus. Er trogt yiddishe tzorrus oifen hartz.* This Jew feels the exile. He carries the Jewish nation's problems in his heart."

An interesting comment, Eliyahu reflected, by someone who fits the same description!

Once, when Eliyahu was learning in Bais Medrash Govoha in Lakewood, N.J., he was talking to Rabbi Aharon Kotler when the Kopicznitzer Rebbe walked in. Reb Aharon immediately jumped up, ran around the table and kissed the Rebbe. Reb Aharon would often say that the Kopicznitzer Rebbe was the pillar of *chessed* in our generation.

■ ■ ■

The night before the Rebbe was due to leave, he called Eliyahu over to him.

"*Ersht darft men machen a cheshbon*. First, we have to make a calculation."

The Rebbe then started to count all the family and friends who had been there for the meals at the hotel. He remembered every single person who had come to visit, and exactly how many meals each of them had eaten. Then he gave Eliyahu a large tip for each of them, and thanked him once more for serving them so well during his stay there.

"When will you be returning to *yeshiva* for Elul *zman*?" the Rebbe asked.

"Monday next week is *rosh chodesh*, when the *zman* starts, so I'll probably go at the end of the week."

"You're starting on Monday, and you're only leaving on Thursday? Oh, that's no good. You need time to rest a bit, so you can go back to *yeshiva* like a *mentch*. You're coming with me back to the city tomorrow."

"But I made up with the boss ... " Eliyahu protested.

"You go pack," the Rebbe said. "I'll work it out with the boss."

Eliyahu packed his bags, then hesitantly went over to his boss.

"The Rebbe..." he began.

"That's okay," his boss interrupted. "I know all about it. The Rebbe already spoke to me, and it's okay for you to go. I'll get someone to replace you for the last few days. And thank you for doing an excellent job!"

It wasn't until their trip the next morning that Eliyahu realized what a *chessed* the Rebbe had done for him by taking him along. Normally, between waiting for buses and actual travel time, it would have taken Eliyahu fourteen hours to get to the city. But the rebbe had arranged for two limousines to take his entire family to a train, and they got to the city in just four hours.

While they were on the train, the Rebbe called him over.

"Elya, you are going back to your mother. You know

your mother is a widow. Did you buy her a gift?"

Eliyahu shook his head. "I didn't think of it," he admitted.

"Elya, I know someone over on the East Side who sells silver. I'll write you a note to take with you, saying that you are a friend of mine. He'll take good care of you and give you a good price."

Once again, Eliyahu was overwhelmed by the Rebbe's fatherly concern. He took an emotional leave of the Rebbe, thanking him for everything he had taught him and all that he had done for him.

A PLACE TWICE YIELDED

Yehoshua,[15] a young *yeshiva* student learning in Lithuania, often dreamed of meeting the legendary Reb Aharon Kotler, the fiery *rosh yeshiva* in Kletzk. What a *zechus* it would be to meet such a lion of Torah face to face!

Once, he asked a friend of his who had seen Reb Aharon, "Tell me, if I would meet Reb Aharon by chance on a train, how would I be able to recognize him?"

The friend smiled. "Simple," he replied. "If you see a man with blue fire burning in his eyes, you will know it is Reb Aharon."

Years went by and the Nazis came to power. Jews throughout Eastern Europe frantically scrambled to find

---

[15] *Name is fictitious.*

means of refuge and escape from the terrible German onslaught. Yehoshua was one of the many *yeshiva bachurim* who rushed to Kovno in an effort to obtain a visa to leave the country.

Once he arrived in Kovno, Yehoshua made his way to the visa office. He was hardly surprised to find a line of people waiting their turn to talk to the consul, but he was dismayed at the size of the line. There were literally dozens and dozens of people in front of him. Yehoshua had no choice but to take his place in line and wait.

Hours passed. Yehoshua tried to tell himself that all these other people were also trying to save their lives, but he couldn't help growing more and more anxious as the line hardly moved. All those people before him would get their visas, but would he? Who knew how many visas would be issued? What would he do if they ran out of visas before his turn arrived?

Yehoshua felt himself beginning to panic. I must get a visa! he thought over and over. I must get out of this terrible country! Desperately, he tried to push himself forward, longing to be at least a few inches closer to the head of the line and potential safety.

A young man standing in front of Yehoshua turned around inquiringly. Yehoshua flushed, embarrassed with his impetuous behavior. Then, without a word, the young man stepped aside and gestured for Yehoshua to take the place in front of him.

As Yehoshua slowly stepped forward, he glanced at the young man with awe. Such an act was true *mesiras nefesh*. Who could this young man be? He, too, was surely desperate to receive a visa and escape the Nazi menace. What kind of nobility did this young man possess that allowed him to act in such a selfless manner?

Yehoshua finally reached the head of the line. Minutes later, he was holding a precious visa in his trembling hands. He was glad to see that the noble young man who had offered him his place was able to receive a visa, too.

Later, Yehoshua discovered that the young man was none other than Reb Shneur Kotler, Reb Aharon's son. He marvelled at the thought of the *gadlus* of Reb Shneur's character. If such was the nobility of the son, imagine what the father must be like!

After the war, Yehoshua made his way to America and joined Bais Medrash Govoha in Lakewood, where he studied under the tutelage of Reb Aharon. It was tremendously gratifying for him to be able to study under the great *rosh yeshiva* after so many years of longing to see the *gadol* and learn from him.

Then darkness struck. Reb Aharon was *niftar*.

Yehoshua's body shook with sobs as he made his way to the small room where Reb Aharon's *aron* lay. He would no longer be able to listen to his *rebbe's* words of wisdom, no longer be able to watch the fire of Torah snapping from his eyes. But at least he could spend a little more time with Reb Aharon, even it was only by saying *tehillim* by his *aron!*

Yehoshua was not the only one who wanted to snatch a few last minutes with the *gadol hador.* The tiny room was packed with students and disciples, all saying *tehillim* and crying uncontrollably. There didn't seem to be any room for Yehoshua at all.

Without thinking, Yehoshua began to push his way into the room. As he tried to find a small space near the *aron,* one man glanced up and moved aside, giving up his place. Grateful, Yehoshua glanced at the man's face. Then he froze. It was Reb Shneur! Once again, Reb Shneur had given up his rightful place for another.

Computer Match

Heshy Schonfeld[16] was dissatisfied. While he was making a good living selling top–quality closeout merchandise, he felt that there had to be more to life than just earning a livelihood. His business took up so much of his time, surely there had to be a way to do *mitzvos* and help others while he was at work!

After much thinking, Heshy hit on a plan. Why not start a toy *gemach* (free loan organization)? He would provide the merchandise, and anyone who couldn't afford to buy toys for his children could simply come to the *gemach* and take one for free.

No sooner said than done! Heshy immediately contacted the *rabbonim* and other prominent people in his area and explained what he was planning to do.

"If you know of anyone who needs this service," he concluded, "please refer them to me!"

One morning, Heshy received a call from Rabbi Lefkowitz.

"I have a wonderful opportunity for the toy *gemach*," Rabbi Lefkowitz told him. "There's a young child, about five years old, who is in a state of chronic depression. He hasn't smiled since the age of one. Anyway, he recently asked his mother to get him a computerized speller. The parents simply can't afford the fifty dollars to buy the computer. Would you be able to help out?"

"Of course! Thank you so much for telling me about this. I'll take care of it right away."

---

[16] *All names are fictitious*

The spelling computer was one item that Heshy had never dealt with in his business, but he didn't hesitate. He gave his secretary fifty dollars and sent her off to the nearest toy store to buy the computer.

A few days later, Rabbi Lefkowitz was back on the phone.

"Heshy, you're not going to believe this. Your gift has literally turned the child into a different person. He began to smile and is acting completely normal. You saved his life!"

Heshy felt both humbled and grateful for this experience. He thanked Hashem for giving him the opportunity to make such a difference in the life of a child.

Some weeks later, Heshy was on a regular business trip, visiting one of his manufacturers to purchase some merchandise for his business. The manufacturer was busy listing the various items he had for sale.

"I've got something a little different this time," he remarked. "I have a whole shipment of computer spellers, eight thousand in all, that are available for a really terrific price. They normally run at thirty to forty dollars, but I'll give them to you for five dollars apiece."

"Five dollars!" Heshy exclaimed in astonishement. "That's incredible! Why hasn't anyone else taken this?"

"I don't know," the manufacturer admitted. "It doesn't make sense to me either. All I can think of is that they don't know exactly what it is, and they just don't want to be bothered with something new."

Heshy hesitated for a moment. Perhaps the other franchisers were right, and it would end up being a bad investment. But then he thought about what the computer had done for that child. Surely many people could benefit from this toy!

"I'll take them all," he said.

Heshy never regretted his decision. Within a short time, he had sold all the computers at eighteen dollars apiece, making a profit of over a hundred thousand dollars.

Clearly, this was nothing less than Divine approval.

FATHERLY LOVE

HaGaon HaRav Shlomo Zalman Auerbach, zt"l (1910–1995), the great Torah leader and posek hador, was also known for his fatherly love and concern for all of Klal Yisrael.

R' Yaakov Landman beamed as he accepted congratulations from his many friends. His wife had just given birth to twin boys, and there were many arrangements to be made before the *brissim* could take place. R' Yaakov also had many questions; after all, he had never been in this situation before! So R' Yaakov made his way to Reb Shlomo Zalman to ask his advice.

Among his many questions, R' Yaakov asked, "Should both children be there together at the *bris*, or should they be brought in one at a time?"

"How could you bring in both children at the same time?" Reb Shlomo Zalman asked in wonderment. "The second child will hear his brother's crying, and share his pain."

And when R' Yaakov left, it was with an indelible impression of Reb Shlomo Zalman's fatherly love for every Jew.

■ ■ ■

Thirteen years later, the time had arrived for the twins to be *bar mitzva*. R' Yaakov invited Reb Shlomo Zalman to come share in the double *simcha*.

The *bar mitzva* was on a *motzei Shabbos*, and that Sunday, Reb Shlomo Zalman was scheduled to have surgery in Tel Aviv. He would actually be going to the hospital on *motzei Shabbos*. Still, Reb Shlomo Zalman insisted on stopping off at the *bar mitzva* and giving his *mazel tov* wishes, before proceeding to Tel Aviv.

A couple of weeks later, R' Yaakov was driving Reb Shlomo Zalman somewhere. The twins happened to be seated in the backseat, and Reb Shlomo Zalman turned around to greet the new *bar mitzva* boys. "Now that you are both *bar mitzva*, we are all the same!" he commented with a big smile.

■ ■ ■

Reb Shlomo Zalman cared for every Jewish child as if he were his own.

One morning, R' Yaakov's son Yom tov had just finished *davening* in the same *minyan* as Reb Shlomo Zalman. Yom Tov was about to leave, but was still standing there when he noticed Reb Shlomo Zalman also walking out the door.

As he made his way down the steps, Reb Shlomo Zalman noticed a little girl waiting, sitting on the steps of the shul.

"Are you waiting for something?" the Gaon asked her gently.

"This morning is my brother's *bar mitzva*," the girl said tearfully. She showed Reb Shlomo Zalman a bag she was holding. "I have cookies for the *l'chaim*, but I don't know what to do with them."

Indeed, Reb Shlomo Zalman realized, there was a *bar*

mitzva taking place in the *shul*. The children had no father, and there was no one to help them organize the *simcha*. The two were on their own.

Not for long, though. Reb Shlomo Zalman took the cookies from the little girl and went back into the *shul*. Then he went up to the *bima* and banged on the table.

"There is a *l'chaim* in honor of the *bar mitzva* boy," he announced.

Reb Shlomo Zalman spread the cookies out on the table himself. He sat the *bar mitzva* boy next to him, taking the place of his father, exchanging *mazel tov* wishes and making the *simcha* one he would long remember.

■ ■ ■

Eleven year old Yom Tov would take the bus to *yeshiva* every morning, and come back home in the afternoon. Since the bus did not go directly to his home in Shaarei Chesed, Yom Tov had a five minute walk at the end of his bus ride. But in the afternoons, he was often accompanied on this walk by Reb Shlomo Zalman, who was returning from Yeshiva Kol Torah to his home, just a short distance from Yom Tov's house. Despite the difference in their ages, Reb Shlomo Zalman always walked together with Yom Tov, sharing thoughts of Torah.

Once, Reb Shlomo Zalman said, "We say each day at the beginning of *davening*, 'Always be a person who is G–d fearing privately and publicly; acknowledge the truth.'

"The first step, which is most important, is 'Always be a person'–strive to be a person, a *mentch*! 'G–d fearing privately'; -your *yiras Hashem* and *tzidkus* should be kept by you privately; it is not for others to know. And 'publicly,' one should 'acknowledge the truth'-be an *emesdike*

Yid: always be truthful with others."

■ ■ ■

Erev Pesach came out on *Shabbos* one year, which cut short the preparations for the *yom tov* by one day. That evening would be the first night of *Pesach*, when all of Klal Yisrael would be eating the *shmura matza*.

"But not I!" R' Yaakov Landman thought to himself gloomily. He had forgotten to take *challah* from his *matzos* before *Shabbos*, and he knew that he couldn't do it on *Shabbos*. R' Yaakov couldn't imagine that there might be a solution to his problem. Still, he sent his son off to Reb Shlomo Zalman for advice.

The answer he received demonstrated Reb Shlomo Zalman's love and concern for every Jew.

"Tell your father he has nothing to worry about," Reb Shlomo Zalman told the boy. "When I took off *challah* from my matzos, I had everyone [who forgot to do it] in mind."[17]

MIRROR IMAGE

R' Yosef Chaim Sonnenfeld, zt"l (1848–1932), Rav of Yerushalayim, used to relate the following story, which he had heard from the great and pious R' Nochum Shadiker.[18]

---

[17] *Yoreh Deah* 328, *Sefer Leket Haomer* 10:5, *Minchas Yitzchok* 4:59
[18] Adapted from the sefer *Maaseh Niflaos*

In R' Nochum's youth, there lived a man named Berel[19] who had strayed from the ways of Hashem and His Torah. Berel's crimes were many, but one of his worst deeds was that of being a *moser*, an informer to the authorities. He constantly got his fellow Jews into trouble. At times, it cost them large sums of money to bribe Berel or to save those already informed upon, who were often sentenced to death.

Understandably, the townspeople greatly feared Berel. They did their best to quickly comply with whatever he wished. And he took advantage of their fear. It was not unusual for Berel to take clothing or utensils from the stores without paying for them. This also happened on market day, when people from neighboring villages would come into town to display and sell their wares. Berel would not hesitate to take whatever he pleased, with never a thought of paying for the merchandise.

But being able to obtain whatever he liked did not satisfy Berel. He also wanted honor. He expected the people to treat him as they would an honorable, learned man. Every *Shabbos*, he demanded that he be given *shishi* when reading the Torah.

The only one who did not join in this universal fear of Berel was the *rav* of the town. The townspeople were very careful not to mention a word about Berel's actions in the presence of the *rav*. They feared that if the *rav* were to hear about Berel's misbehavior, he would do anything he could to stop Berel in his tracks and convince him to return to the Torah. Knowing Berel, they felt certain he would pour out his anger on their *rav*. And so the townspeople remained silent.

One early morning, a Jew from a small, faraway village

---

[19] *Name is fictitious*

came into town for market day. He brought with him the fruits of his field and other merchandise to sell. He thought it important to come very early in the morning, while most people were still asleep. This way, he would arrive before the regular dealers, and there would be a chance that people would buy from him.

The man began to set up his wagon, laying out all the fruits and produce in an attractive manner. As he worked, he noticed a well dressed, distinguished–looking man approaching. The customer scrutinized his wares, then began picking out the best of the produce. The dealer was very excited at the amount of food that the man was taking. Why, even if this were his only customer of the day, he would still make a handsome profit!

The customer finished making his selections, and the dealer stood by with a smile, waiting to take the customer's money. Bu this smile turned to a frown as the man began to walk away without paying for his purchases.

"Excuse me, sir," the dealer called. "You forgot to pay."

The customer stopped in his tracks. He turned back to the dealer with a scowl and snapped, "You're asking *me* for money? Everyone gives me everything for free! What makes you think that you're any different from the rest of the people?"

The dealer could not believe his ears. He grabbed the customer by the collar and yelled, "Thief! You'd better pay me for my property!"

"Don't be foolish," the man responded calmly. "I am well known here in town. Go ahead, ask the townspeople about Reb Berel. They'll tell you who I am. Believe me, if you continue to treat me this way, you'll regret it."

With that, Berel shook off the dealer and nonchalantly continued on his way.

The dealer wasn't going to put up with that kind of behavior. He asked around until he discovered where the *rav* lived, then went there quickly to present his case.

It was still early, and the *rav's* family and assistants were not yet awake. And so it happened that it was the *rav* himself who heard the man's knocking and opened the door to let him in.

The dealer related to the *rav* exactly what had happened. The *rav* was very surprised. "That man is very honored here in town. They give him great respect. As a matter of fact, every *Shabbos* he receives *shishi* in *shul*. I'm sure there is some explanation for this. Let me call him here to my house, and we'll get to the bottom of this episode."

As the *rav* finished speaking to the dealer, his assistant entered the room, ready to begin the day's work. The *rav* turned to him. "Please call Reb Berel to my house immediately."

The assistant looked at the *rav*, who appeared very perturbed, and then at the dealer, who was standing at the *rav's* side. His heart sank as he realized that the truth was about to come out.

"It's a bit early to call him here now. Perhaps the *rav* can see Reb Berel after *davening*? Everyone is waiting for the *rav* to begin *davening*."

"No, no, you must call him immediately. This Jew here must go home soon, and it is not right to make him wait."

The assistant fearfully went to comply with the *rav's* request. As he came before Berel, he began to shake.

"The r–r–rav asked," he stuttered, "perhaps your respected honor would be so kind and come to the *rav* for a moment? He has something to discuss with your honor."

Berel knew quite well why the *rav* wanted to speak with him. And he had no intention of complying.

"Go tell the *rav* that I am not coming," he said curtly. "I have nothing to discuss with him."

The assistant quickly returned to the *rav*. "Ah, Reb Berel says that he is unable to come to the *rav* now. He is sorry that he is unable to comply with the *rav's* request."

"Return to Reb Berel," the *rav* said firmly. "Tell him that he must come *now*."

The assistant returned to Berel. "The *rav* has asked for your honor to come to his house right now."

"Is that so?" Berel sneered. "Tell the *rav* not to interfere in something that is not his concern."

Once again, the assistant returned to the *rav* and relayed the message. After hearing Berel's latest refusal, the *rav* turned to the dealer at his side.

"Please be patient. I will make sure that the money owed is given to you. In the meantime, you can return home. I will be in touch with you."

It wasn't long before the entire town was talking about the episode. "Perhaps we should explain to the *rav* just who Reb Berel really is," some people suggested. "Maybe if he understands the whole story, he'll look the other way, so the whole town won't have to suffer."

But as far as Berel was concerned, it was too late for apologies. The *rav*, he decided, had overstepped his authority, and it was high time for Reb Berel to show him who was really in charge in this town. That *Shabbos*, he put his plan into action.

Berel approached the *gabbai* before *davening*. "I want you to make a change in the usual system," he declared. "I want you to call me up for *shlishi* instead of the *rav*, and give the *rav* my usual *shishi*."

Now the *gabbai*, along with everyone else, was scared of Berel, and usually went out of his way to please him. This time, though, Berel had gone too far. The *gabbai's* respect for the *tzaddik* won out over his fear of the *rasha*, and he called up the *rav* for *shlishi* as usual.

When it was time for *shishi*, the *gabbai* called up Berel. But now the *rav* intervened. He went up to the *bima* and declared, "Someone else must be called up for *shishi*."

Berel, who was already in place, refused to move. The other person came up for *shishi*, and Berel pushed him away.

The *rav* strode up to Berel and slapped him in the face.

Berel reeled in shock. But then his hand reached out, and it slapped against the *rav's* cheek.

The people were shocked into silence. For a moment they stood watching the appalling tableau, as Berel and the *rav* seemed frozen into immobility.

And then the moment passed. Berel stormed out of *shul*, shouting, "You'll all be sorry! Not one of you stood up to help me. Every last one of you will suffer!"

The uproar spread throughout the whole town. People whispered the news to each other, and it wasn't long before two groups had formed, each in support of their own candidate. One group supported the *rav's* position to do as he saw fit. The other group, while realizing that the *rav* was right, was afraid of the repercussions that would result if Berel was not appeased.

That group quickly made its way to Berel's house, where the informer was still fuming at the way he had been treated. Eventually, they managed to calm him down somewhat.

"All right," Berel finally said grudgingly. "I won't get even with the whole town. But that doesn't apply to the *rav*! I'm still going to get him."

The townspeople who supported the *rav* were naturally concerned for him. They appointed two of his students, one of whom was R' Nochum Shadiker, to always stay at his side and protect him, day and night.

One day, an unknown messenger came to the *rav*, inviting him to be the *sandek* at a *bris* that would be taking place in a nearby town. The *rav* agreed to go, and the next morning, he and his students entered the wagon that was to take them to the *bris*.

The wagon was some distance down the road when the students suddenly noticed some dangerous looking men approaching in the distance. As the men came closer, they realized that one of the people in the group was Berel.

"What should we do?" one of the students moaned. He looked to the *rav* for advice, but the *tzaddik* was completely immersed in his learning and he hadn't noticed a thing.

The other student spoke directly to the *rav*. "I am sorry for disturbing the *rav*, but there are some dangerous men coming toward us on the road."

The *rav* lifted his head and gazed at the approaching men. His face remained calm as he returned to his learning, as if he had no other concerns.

The students, however, remained tense as the wagon drew closer. They thought about Berel, the source of their danger. "That wicked man!" they thought to themselves. "If only we could destroy him!"

When Berel finally reached the wagon, the students prepared themselves for a fight. But then an amazing thing happened.

Berel came face to face with the *rav*. He stood looking silently at the *rav* for a moment. The look of anger on his face slowly faded away, to be replaced by one of awe and love.

And then he spoke.

"Please forgive me, *rebbe*, for my sins against you. I just ask for one thing. Please let me take my revenge against these two men who are accompanying you."

"These are my students," the *rav* said. "You have no reason to bear a grudge against them."

The *rav* then began to admonish Berel for all of the evil deeds that he had done in the past. Berel broke down crying, expressing regret for all his actions and promising to return to Hashem's ways. The *rav* and his students then peacefully continued on their way.

As soon as they were alone, the students ask the *rav* to explain to them how this amazing occurrence had taken place.

"When we were in danger," the *rav* explained, "I began to think about where in the Torah I could find a lesson that taught me how to act in this situation. I thought of the time when Yaakov met up with Eisav. Yaakov tried to rid himself of all his anger and hate toward Eisav. As it says in *Mishlei* (27:19), 'Just as water reflects a person's face, so does a person's face reflect what another feels toward him.' If a person shows goodness of heart toward his friend, that friend will reciprocate that goodness of heart. Yaakov understood that if he would show goodness of heart to Eisav, then Eisav would treat him in the same way.

"That is exactly what I did. I began judging Reb Berel favorably. He is not completely at fault for his evil ways; we are all at fault, for bowing to his actions instead of reproving him. I continued thinking in this fashion until all the hate had left my heart. And so when he saw me, all the hate also left his heart, and he treated me in that fashion.

"You two, however, continued to feel hate and anger for him. And so he felt the same way toward you."

Bubble Gum

The following story was told by Mrs. B. Versicherter of Lakewood, New Jersey.

The room was filled with chattering girls as the sixth grade class of Bezalel Hebrew Day School, Lakewood, N.J., entered their classroom. It was *berachos* bee time, and their teacher, Mrs. Weinstein, had assigned a *berachos* collage as a project. Every girl had worked very hard on her collage, and today they would finally be unveiled.

Mrs. Weinstein walked into the room, and the girls quickly quieted down.

"All right, girls, we're going to present our projects one by one to the rest of the class."

Ilana waited eagerly in her seat. She, too, had worked hard on her project, and she couldn't wait to show it to her teacher.

"Okay, Ilana, it's your turn. Let's see what you've done!"

Ilana proudly brought up her collage. She had put a lot of work into it, and she could tell that her teacher was impressed with her collection.

Mrs. Weinstein studied the project carefully. Ilana had really done an excellent job. There was just one thing . . . But that would wait until after class.

"Terrific, Ilana! You really worked hard on this. Beautiful job!"

Ilana went beaming back to her seat, and the rest of the presentations continued.

Time went by quickly, and the bell rang, signalling the end of class.

"All right, girls, you're dismissed . . . Ilana, can I speak to you for a minute?"

The rest of the class left the room, some girls glancing curiously back at Ilana as they walked out the door. Ilana, too, was curious. As soon as her classmates left, she walked over to her teacher's desk.

"What is it, Mrs. Weinstein?"

"Ilana, you really did a beautiful job. I can see how much work you put into this project, and I'm very impressed.

"There's just one thing I'm curious about. What is this gum wrapper that you used for *shehakol*?"

"That? Why, that's the gum I always chew. The *beracha* on gum is *shehakol*, right?"

"The *beracha* on gum is *shehakol*, Ilana," Mrs. Weinstein said gently. "But is that gum kosher?"

Ilana blinked in surprise. "Why, I don't know. I never even thought about it."

"Okay, Ilana." Mrs. Weinstein smiled warmly. "I don't want to keep you, so go ahead now."

The next day, Mrs. Weinstein called Ilana over before class.

"Here, Ilana, I brought you something."

She dropped a little bag into her student's hand. Ilana opened it curiously.

Inside were three packages of kosher chewing gum.

"What's this for?" she asked in surprise.

"It's kosher chewing gum. I thought you might like to try some."

Ilana smiled and thanked her teacher for her thoughtfulness. She had gone out of her way to get Ilana the kosher chewing gum, while making sure that she didn't embarrass Ilana in the process.

A year later a terrible tragedy occurred. Mrs. Yehudis Weinstein and her husband Yonah were killed in a car accident. Many of Mrs. Weinstein's students were devastated by the news, and Ilana could find no peace within herself.

After the tragedy, many people came to the school to speak about Mrs. Weinstein. Several suggested that the students accept upon themselves to do one *mitzva* in their teacher's memory. But Ilana was unable to think of anything that seemed appropriate.

Suddenly she remembered the episode with the kosher gum.

"That's it!" Ilana decided. "From this day on, I will only eat kosher gum. This *mitzva* that I do should be a merit for Mrs. Weinstein."

As the years passed, Ilana's undertaking has led her to accept more and more *mitzvos*. Today, both she and her family have grown in following the ways of Hashem and His Torah. No doubt the love and concern Mrs. Weinstein showed to Ilana left its mark and inspiration.

3

NOBLE ATTRIBUTES

A Blessed Shidduch

■ ■ ■

Solid Investment

■ ■ ■

A Holy Nation

■ ■ ■

Revolving Kindness

■ ■ ■

Bakeries and Bar-Mitzvahs

■ ■ ■

Good Evening

■ ■ ■

The Right Time

■ ■ ■

I Was So Sure

■ ■ ■

Family Ties

3
Noble Attributes

A Blessed Shidduch

Menachem Kerper[20] sat spellbound in the audience, listening to the Ponovezher Rav, Reb Yosef Shlomo Kahaneman zt"l (1886–1969). The Rav had come to England to raise funds for his *yeshiva* in Bnei Brak.

Menachem was captivated by the words of this tremendous *tzaddik*. Somehow, he thought, I must find a way to serve the Rav! With trepidation, he approached the Rav after the lecture and asked if he could serve him in any way. To Menachem's great delight, his services were accepted.

---

[20] *Name is fictitious*

Menachem accompanied the Rav on his fundraising drive, giving his assistance wherever it was required. When the Rav's mission was finally complete, and he was ready to return to Israel, Menachem approached him one last time.

"Can the Rav give me a blessing?"

"What blessing would you like to have?" the Rav asked him.

Menachem thought for a moment. In his late thirties, Menachem was still unmarried, and his first idea had been to ask the Rav for a blessing in finding a *shidduch*. But then Menachem changed his mind.

"Rebbe, please bless me that I should merit to have good, G-d fearing children."

The request did seem a bit strange. But the Rav nevertheless complied, and blessed Menachem wholeheartedly.

Months passed. *Rosh Hashana* came and went. When *Yom Kippur* arrived, Menachem was, as usual, praying in *shul* together with his father. The *mincha* prayer approached, and the congregation, according to its custom, began offering bids for *Maftir Yonah* and the *Pesicha* for *Neilah*.

As the bidding began, Menachem was struck by an idea. Why not bid for one of these honors to give to his father? Menachem knew that his father was a descendent of Torah scholars, and he was aware that his grandfather used to acquire these honors every year on *Yom Kippur*.

The price for *Maftir Yonah* was high. Menachem was a working man, but times were hard, and he knew he couldn't afford it. Instead, he tried for the honor of *Pesicha*.

The bidding seemed to be going well for Menachem. But there was one man, Rabbi Kershenbaum, who kept topping Menachem's bids. Rabbi Kershenbaum was actually not a regular member of the congregation. He was an Israeli who had come to London to raise money, but for some reason, he was very determined to win the honor himself.

Menachem found himself bidding beyond his means. But a natural stubborness kept him from giving in, and he kept going, raising the price even higher. Finally, the bidding reached an exorbitant amount, and Rabbi Kershenbaum dropped out. The honor belonged to Menachem.

Menachem proudly ran over to his father and presented the honor to him. But his joy quickly turned to dismay when his father told him to hand the honor over to Rabbi Kershenbaum! Menachem was confused and hurt. But he hid his feelings well, and handed the honor over to Rabbi Kershenbaum, who couldn't help being impressed by Menachem's action.

After *Yom Kippur*, Rabbi Kershenbaum traveled to Liverpool. He hoped to get an American visa, as well as continue his fundraising. Unfortunately, Rabbi Kershenbaum did not speak English very well, and he found his efforts hampered at every turn.

Someone in the Jewish community offered to help. He introduced Rabbi Kershenbaum to a young boy from another family in the community.

"David[21] here is willing to help you out. Take him along with you."

Rabbi Kershenbaum set off on his errands with David in tow. As the day progressed, he grew more and more grateful to this young man, who assisted him in every possible way. When the day came to an end, Rabbi Kershenbaum thanked his young helper profusely.

"Is there any *beracha* I can give you in return?" he asked.

David thought for a moment. "There's nothing I need

---

[21] *Name is fictitious*

personally. But I do have an older sister who isn't married, and I really would like to find a *shidduch* for her."

Rabbi Kershenbaum smiled. "As it happens, I know of a terrific young man. During *Yom Kippur* I was in London, and I met a remarkable young man there. Menachem Kerper is quite a few years older than your sister, but he is a *ben Torah* from a nice family, and I know first hand that he is a very charitable person."

Rabbi Kershenbaum went on to describe what had happened in *shul* that *Yom Kippur*. David actually had known Menachem from before, since the families had grown up together. He was impressed now by what Rabbi Kershenbaum had told him, and a meeting between the two young people was arranged.

Not long after, Menachem and David's sister were married. The Ponovezher Rav's blessing came true, as Menachem and his wife today enjoy the gift of their G–d fearing children and grandchildren.

A Solid Investment

1973 was a good year for Eliezer Mendelsohn. Not only did he get married, but he also started working for his father–in–law, Velvel Bernstein, a man who, he soon discovered, was far more than an ordinary businessman.

Velvel Bernstein was a wholesale distributor of toys, and at the time that his son–in–law began working for him, his was an established and well–regarded firm. It also happened to be the only firm of its size to be closed on *Shabbos* and *yom tov*.

One day, Velvel called his son-in-law into his office for a chat.

"I'd like to show you something about how I run my business. I am about to make a wrong business decision, but it is, at the same time, a correct ethical decision."

Eliezer was intrigued. "What exactly do you mean?"

"Before I explain what I'm talking about," Velvel said with a smile, "let me tell you about how my business got its first big break."

Velvel explained that the first major discount center on the West Coast had been a retail chain called White Front. "They were the first to make the transition from a small, independent variety chain to a mass merchant discount center. They were very much ahead of their time. As you can imagine, they were also very aggressive."

It was this company that had given Velvel's business the chance to make the leap from an average sized company to a large production business. "One of their purchasers, a man named Harry Blackman, called me one day and asked me to supply him with merchandise for the big season. I knew this was a great opportunity, so I did everything I possibly could to fill his order. We did the job, and they were happy.

"Shortly afterwards, Harry asked me if I had done well filling their order. When I told him that I had, he said that he had been very happy with the production, and that he wanted to expand the business even more. Naturally, that meant more business for me.

"Eventually, White Front sold out to a company called Interstate. But they continued to work closely with me. And as their business grew, so did mine."

But the discount center market soon became crowded. More competitors came on the scene, and Interstate began to take a beating. They suffered many losses, and soon it was rumored that they were on the verge of financial collapse.

By this time, Velvel's business had become well known. He had many other customers, and he was no longer dependent on Interstate's business. So when Interstate called him the following year, asking for credit so they could rebuild themselves, Velvel knew that he would be taking a chance.

"I have no sound justification for giving them credit," Velvel told Eliezer. "Chances are that they won't make it, and I'll never see a penny of the money. But I owe them a debt of gratitude. When I needed to expand, they were there to give me that break. Their assistance helped bring about my success.

"My accountant tells me not to do it," Velvel concluded, "but nevertheless, I will be giving them the goods on credit. I owe it to them, and I feel that this is what Hashem would want me to do."

Velvel was as good as his word. He gave the credit, then sadly watched when Interstate went bankrupt at the end of the season. Velvel lost $82,000 on the deal, but he had no regrets. He felt sure that he had done what was right. He wrote off the money as a bad debt and that, he thought, was the end of it.

A year passed. Another toy company formed out of the ashes of the Interstate bankruptcy. Since they wanted to stay on good terms with the vendors in the toy trade, they decided to pay back all of Interstate's old debts.

Velvel was surprised when he got the call.

"We'd like to repay the $82,000," they told him.

Caught off guard, Velvel stammered, "But I've already written it off as a bad debt!"

"But we'd really like to clear up all the old debts," they insisted. "What about accepting stock in our new company for the value of the debt?"

Velvel agreed to that idea. He was issued the stock, but he never bothered looking at it or doing anything with it. As far as he was concerned, the issue was closed.

It wasn't until four years later that Velvel took the stocks out again. This time, he decided to sell them. The stock? Toys 'R' Us. The value? One million, seven hundred thousand dollars.

A Holy Nation

Meir Ament knocked on the door to his employer's office.

"Hi, Meir, come on in. What's up?"

"Listen, I just thought of a great opportunity," Meir told his boss, settling himself down in a chair in front of the oak-panelled desk.

Meir worked as a salesman for a souvenir company in Montreal, Canada. He was always on the lookout for new ideas, and now he decided that he had come up with a winner.

"Why don't we try selling our T-shirts at Niagara Falls?" he asked his boss.

"I don't know, Meir. It's a great market, but it's pretty hard to break into it. They've probably been using the same suppliers for years."

"That's true," Meir acknowledged, "but it doesn't hurt to try. If it works, we could make a lot of money on this."

"Okay, Meir, give it a shot. It's all yours!"

The next few days found Meir doing a lot of research on the Niagara Falls souvenier market. The stores in that area were all government owned, and there was one man who was in charge of making all the purchases for those stores. Eventually, Meir tracked down Lee Ryan[22] and made an appointment to see him.

Meir walked into Mr. Ryan's office wearing the hat and jacket he always wore, just as he had done in his *yeshiva* days. Mr. Ryan welcomed him in and waved him to a seat.

"You can take off your hat and just wear your *yarmulka* here," the manager told him.

Meir was taken aback. He wasn't expecting that type of statement from a non–Jew. He wasn't sure whether to comment on the incident or not, so he decided to sail right into his sales pitch.

Mr. Ryan listened to Meir without comment. After only a short time, he interrupted the salesman.

"Look, why should I buy from you? There are plenty of suppliers here who we have been working with for years, and who do a good job. Why should we start with someone new?"

"Well, we really have terrific products ..."

Meir tried to continue the sales pitch, but he didn't feel that he was getting across to Mr. Ryan. The manager continued to look unimpressed.

"Thanks for coming down," he said, when Meir finally finished. "If we're interested, we'll let you know."

Meir left the office in discouragement. He had done his best, but unfortunately, he felt that it simply hadn't been good enough this time.

No one was more surprised than Meir when, two months later, his company received an order from Mr. Ryan for twelve thousand T–shirts. A year later, Meir, feeling much

---

[22] *Name is fictitious.*

more confident, went back to Mr. Ryan to show his wares. This time, he ordered 150,000 T-shirts.

Every year the amount of the order increased steadily, and every year Meir thanked Hashem for giving him this account. Meir did wonder what had caused Mr. Ryan to decide to order from their company. After all, their initial meeting hadn't really gone that well, but he never had the courage to ask.

For ten years, Mr. Ryan ordered from Meir's company. During all that time, the manager never came down to visit the company in person. Then, one year, Meir received a phone call from Mr. Ryan.

"I'm coming to Montreal next week, and I'd like to visit your company."

"Of course! We'd be delighted to have you here."

"Great. And would you mind taking me out for a kosher meal?"

The request seemed a bit odd to Meir, but he had no trouble with it. As the two of them sat over their dinners in a kosher restaurant, Mr. Ryan gave Meir a thoughtful look.

"You know, I'd like to tell you a story.

"I was born and bred in London, England. I was only nine years old during the war, and my parents sent me to Canada for safety. They gave me the name and address of a relative who offered to take care of me, and then sent me off on my own.

"Imagine my despair when I arrived in Canada and discovered that the person they had told me about did not exist! There was no one by that name, and there was no such address, either. I wandered the streets all alone, with nowhere to go.

"It was wartime then, and no one could afford to take care of a homeless child. I entered a few shops in the hope of finding some work to do, but no one was interested.

"Then one morning, I saw a sign over a store that had the word 'Scottish' on it. For some reason, I decided to try my luck in there. The man inside was wearing a Jewish head covering. I told him about what had happened to me. Finally, I had found someone who truly sympathized with a lonely, abandoned child. He offered me a cup of hot tea and a place to rest. He gave me as much help as he could.

"When I left, I swore that one day I would repay him for the warmth and solace he had given me at a time when I needed it most. Years later, when I became successful, I did find that man again, and I gave him a lot of business.

"When you came to me ten years ago with your black hat and jacket, I saw that you were also a religious Jew. Why not give your company a try? I thought. And when I saw that your company did a good job, I increased the order every year."

Meir thanked Mr. Ryan for sharing his secret with him. And he thanked Hashem for giving him the privilege of being a part of His holy people. The man who had helped a poor lonely boy so many years ago had no idea of the great *kiddush Hashem* he was performing, or of the fruit it would bear in years to come.

Revolving Kindness

R' Yaakov Koff (Kavkewetz) was a *talmid* in the original Mirrer Yeshiva in Europe. After the war, he made his way to America, where he became a *mashgiach* of several butcher shops and the *baal koreh* in the Young Israel of Spring Valley.

One year, a few months before *Sukkos*, R' Yaakov went into the hospital for a minor surgical procedure. When the procedure was over, R' Yaakov felt very weak, but the doctor reassured him that this was normal.

"Don't worry. Tomorrow you'll be just fine," R' Yaakov was told.

The following morning, R' Yaakov's son, Zvi, was walking toward his father's room to visit him when he noticed his father's doctor leaving the room.

The doctor stopped him in the hallway.

"I'm afraid I have bad news for you. There seem to have been some complications in the night. I don't think your father's going to make it."

"What are you talking about? This was supposed to be a simple procedure!

"We're not sure what happened. When we came into his room this morning, he wasn't breathing. We managed to revive him, but we don't know if we were there in time."

Zvi was devastated. He simply couldn't believe that the hospital had let this happen. Why hadn't they been taking better care of his father?

The family was understandably upset, as well as insecure about the level of care R' Yaakov was receiving in the hospital. They insisted that a specialist be brought in.

The hospital wasn't pleased, but there was little they could do about it. Still, there was a feeling of ill will between the doctors and the family. The tension was simply causing more aggravation in an already tense situation.

At this point, a close friend of the Koff family, Rabbi Avraham Gendel, stepped in. Rabbi Gendel was a *rebbe* in Mesivta Beis Shraga and the rabbi of Young Israel of Spring Valley, where Rabbi Koff was the *baal koreh*. He interceded for the family with the hospital and made sure that they were spared any additional aggravation. He tried to clear the way for the specialist so R' Yaakov would get the expert medical attention that he needed.

Fortunately, R' Yaakov's condition began to improve. He was still in intensive care, but there were signs that he would come out of his coma. Finally, after a month in a coma, he was released from intensive care.

The family's happiness, however, was shaken by another tragedy. On the same day that Rabbi Koff was released from intensive care, Rabbi Gendel had a massive heart attack and passed away.

Rabbi Koff eventually recuperated completely and went home. Two years later, however, he became ill, and he passed away on *chol hamoed Sukkos*.

His son, Yitzchok, accompanied the *aron* to Israel. The family had already spoken with several prominent *rabbonim* about finding a respectable place to put their father to rest. The *rabbonim* suggested one specific place on Har Hazeisim.

Near the end of the funeral, an old friend of R' Yaakov's who had learned with him in the Mir spoke up.

"Why isn't your father being buried in the special Mirrer section?" he asked Yitzchok.

Yitzchok was astonished. He hadn't known about a Mirrer section. Why hadn't the *rabbonim* the family had consulted told them about this?

A closer look at the place where his father was buried soon made matters clear. R' Koff had been placed right near his dear friend, Rabbi Avraham Gendel.

■ ■ ■

A few years later, Yitzchok Koff had started a new job in New York City. He had to drive into work from Monsey on *chol hamoed Sukkos*. Since it was the day of his father's *yahrzeit*, he needed to find an early *minyan* where he could lead the *davening* before going into work.

After several inquiries, Yitzchok was directed to a specific *shul*, where he was assured that he wouldn't have any problem. In the morning, he came early to *shul* and asked the rabbi if he could lead the *minyan*.

"You'll have to ask Charlie back there," the rabbi told him. "He also has *yahrzeit* today, but maybe he won't mind sharing the pulpit with you."

Yitzchok quickly went over to Charlie.

"Hello, my name is Yitzchok Koff. The rabbi told me that you have *yahrzeit* today. I, too, have *yahrzeit* today. Would I be able to share leading the *davening* with you?"

Charlie stared at Yitzchok for a moment.

"Who do you have *yahrzeit* for?" he asked Yitzchok finally.

"It's for my father."

"Are you from Spring Valley?"

"Yes, I am."

"And was your father Rabbi Koff from Spring Valley?"

"Yes, that's right."

"In that case, go right ahead. You can lead the *davening* yourself."

With that, Charlie walked away, leaving Yitzchok alone to begin the *davening*.

Yitzchok couldn't understand what had happened. He led the first part of *davening*, but when he had a chance later, during the Torah reading, he again went over to Charlie.

"Why don't you lead the rest of *davening*?" he suggested.

But Charlie shook his head. "No, you do it." And once again he walked away.

After *davening*, Yitzchok walked over to the rabbi to thank him.

"You're welcome," the rabbi said. "But I don't understand why Charlie didn't *daven*. He had already told me that he would lead the *minyan* today. I wonder what made him change his mind?"

Yitzchok, too, was curious. So before Charlie had a chance to leave, he went over to him and asked him straight out.

Charlie looked at Yitzchok thoughtfully. "Let me tell you a little story. Years ago, my mother and I first moved to Spring Valley. We didn't know anyone there. One day, my mother passed away suddenly, and I had no one to turn to. I walked into the Young Israel of Spring Valley, but the place seemed to be empty, save for one man.

"As I said, I had no one else to turn to, so I told this man my story. He was very warm and friendly, and he promised to help me in any way he could. He immediately arranged the funeral and made sure that I had a *minyan* throughout the entire week.

"Soon after that, I moved out of Spring Valley, and I never had the chance to properly thank that man for everything he did for me and my mother.

"That man was your father, Rabbi Yaakov Koff.

"This morning, when I heard your name, I felt that this would be one way I could at least partially express my *hakoras hatov* for what your father did for me."

"Tell me," Yitzchok said curiously, "who did you have *yahrzeit* for today?"

"Today was my mother's *yahrzeit*," Charlie said softly.

BAKERIES AND BAR MITZVAS

The following story was related by Mr. Hirsch Wolf of Brooklyn, New York.

Yossel Hirsch arrived in New York in the late 1940's with nothing more than the shirt on his back. A survivor of World War II, Yossel nevertheless managed to always be cheerful and content, despite the hardships he had lived through. Yossel always had a nice word to say to everyone, and he went out of his way to help and inspire others.

Like all new immigrants, Yossel needed to find a way to support his family. Fortunately, it wasn't long before he found a job working in a bakery. Yossel worked hard. Best of all, he was efficient and honest. He was well liked by both the customers and his employers. Even the vendors who did business with the bakery found Yossel a pleasure to work with.

One day Moshe Kantesky[23], one of the vendors, made his usual delivery. He came into the bakery and lingered until Yossel turned to him with a smile.

"Can I talk to you for a minute, Yossel?" he asked seriously.

"Sure, what is it?"

"I have a suggestion for you. Why don't you go into business for yourself, and open a bakery of your own? You're efficient, and you have a great personality. I'm sure you'd be very successful."

Yossel thanked him warmly. "It's nice of you to say so. In fact, I've considered opening my own business. But there's

---
[23] *Name is fictitious*

really no way I can manage it. I came to this country without any money, and I simply don't have the capital to open my own business."

"That's true," Moshe acknowledged. "But I'm so convinced that you'll be a success that I'm prepared to lend you the money. When you make the money back, you can repay me."

Yossel was taken by surprise. What an incredible opportunity! He accepted the loan of nearly twenty thousand dollars, which, at that time, was an enormous amount of money, and opened his own bakery in a different neighborhood.

Moshe Kantesky proved to be right. Yossel really had the perfect personality for this type of business, and his customers always enjoyed speaking with him as they did their shopping. There were others who had a hard time paying, and he often let them shop for free. Yossel's store became very popular, and before long his business was very successful. Eventually, Yossel made enough money to pay back Moshe, which he did with many heartfelt thanks.

Years went by. An aged Moshe Kantesky passed away from this world, and Yossel wished his good friend a tearful farewell.

One evening, Yossel returned from a hard day's work and fell into a deep sleep. In his dream, Moshe Kantesky was once again standing before him.

"Moshe, what are you doing here? You've already left this world."

"You're right, Yossel, but I need to speak with you. Remember that big favor I did for you, when I lent you the money for the bakery?"

"Of course I remember. How could I ever forget?"

"Well, now I'm the one asking for a favor. I need your help."

"What can I do for you now?" Yossel asked in bewilderment.

"It's my children," Moshe explained. "I left my business to my two sons. Unfortunately, after I died, my business suffered some losses. The two of them did not see eye to eye on many issues, and they began to argue with each other. One thing led to another, and now the families will not speak to one another.

"One of my sons is making a *bar mitzva*, and he didn't invite his brother to attend. I can't begin to tell you how much pain my soul is suffering from this. I have no rest here in the next world. I beg you to help me!"

With that, Moshe disappeared.

Yossel woke in the morning feeling ill at ease. Should he take the dream seriously? Perhaps he should first check to see if there really was bad blood between Moshe's two sons. Yossel began making inquiries, and he soon discovered that his dream had indeed been accurate. Clearly, there was a lot of work to be done before the whole situation could be sorted out.

Yossel began by calling Moshe's older son and reminiscing about the old times, his father and the business.

"Don't talk to me about the business," the son sighed. "All that work my father put into building it up was completely wasted. Thanks to my brother, we nearly lost the whole thing."

"I'm sorry to hear that," Yossel said carefully.

"Yes, well," the son sounded uncomfortable, "I suppose I shouldn't blame my brother completely. These things can happen, I guess. But the whole thing ended up causing a lot of arguments and bad feelings, and today our families aren't on speaking terms.

"But let's talk about more cheerful things. Did you know that I'm making a *bar mitzva* soon? My oldest son!"

"*Mazel tov!*" Yossel congratulated him. "You know, a *simcha* is a perfect time to make amends. Why not take this opportunity to invite your brother and his family?"

"Oh, I couldn't!" was the instant response. "My brother would never agree to come. He's still too upset with me."

Taking a tip from Aharon Hakohen, who was well known for his peace making abilities, Yossel said, "On the contrary! I already spoke to your brother, and he really would like to make amends. He's distressed that the feud is still going on, and he really wishes the families would reunite."

"Really?" the older brother said thoughtfully. "I didn't know that. Well, I'll consider it."

Yossel hung up and then immediately called the younger brother. The conversation followed similar lines, until Yossel brought up the subject of the *bar mitzva*. "Why don't you go to the *simcha*?" he asked.

"I can't have anything to do with that *bar mitzva*," the younger brother said dispiritedly. "I didn't even get an invitation."

"But I spoke to your brother, and he really wishes you would come," Yossel urged. "He didn't send you an invitation because he thought you would never agree to come. But he really would like you to be there."

"My brother said that?" the younger brother said thoughtfully. "Well, I'll consider it."

When the *bar mitzva* night arrived, both brothers arrived at the hall and fell into each other's arms. Finally the families enjoyed a true *simcha*, unmarred by conflict and bad feelings. And Yossel knew that the ultimate *simcha* was taking place in Heaven, as their father watched his two sons, and their families, reunited in complete harmony.

Good Evening

The following story was related by Rav Moshe Aaron Stern, Mashgiach in the Kamenitzer Yeshiva in Yerushalayim.

Recently, the Rabanut Harashut in Yerushalayim began sending G-d-fearing slaughterers to South America. The men slaughtered the animals there, and then sent the kosher meat to Israel.

The slaughterhouse in South America provides excellent accomodations for this purpose, and the entire operation is strictly supervised. Every evening, the owner of the site, Mr. Samo[24], checks over the building, making sure that everything is in order before leaving for the night.

One evening as Mr. Samo walked out of the building, he met Alex[25], the night watchman.

"Are you leaving now, Mr. Samo?" Alex asked. "There's still one slaughterer in the building."

"What do you mean? I was just in there, checking through the building, and I didn't see anyone."

"I'm positive he's still in there," Alex insisted.

"Well, if you say so, I'll check again."

Mr. Samo went back through the building, Again, he found the place empty.

"I checked, Alex, and there's no one there. Maybe he left when you weren't looking."

"Please, Mr. Samo," Alex begged, "I know he's still in there. Maybe there's something wrong and he's in trouble! Could you please check more thoroughly?"

---

[24] *Name is fictitious*
[25] *Name is fictitious*

Mr. Samo was moved by Alex's genuine concern. The night watchman sounded so certain!

"Okay, Alex, I'll check one more time."

Back he went through the building, searching high and low. But Mr. Samo once again found no trace of anyone. Then, just as he was passing by the freezer, a thought struck him.

"What if someone's in there? The freezer is big enough for a person to walk inside. I'll just take a quick look."

Mr. Samo opened the freezer door and found three of the slaughterers inside, nearly frozen. He quickly ran to the phone and called for an ambulance.

The slaughterers had been in the freezer to check on the meat. When they were ready to leave, they had discovered that the door wouldn't open. They had banged and yelled, but there had been no response. Fortunately, Mr. Samo had found them in time. After only a few days in the hospital, they were fully recovered.

Mr. Samo went over to Alex. "How could you possibly have known that someone was still in there? I checked carefully, but you were still so certain! Also, why didn't you tell me that three people were in there? If you knew about one of them, surely you would have known about three of them!"

"Ever since those men came from Israel a few months ago," Alex explained, "one of them always wished me good morning when he came in every day, and good evening when he left at night. He's done this every single day without fail.

"That day, I remembered that he had said hello to me in the morning, but he hadn't wished me a good night. That's how I knew that he, at least, was definitely still in there."

A simple greeting! Mr. Samo reflected. Yet it had saved not only the slaughterer's own life but also the lives of two of his colleagues.

THE RIGHT TIME

"Do not hate your brother in your heart; you must admonish your neighbor..." (Vayikra 19:17) Airing one's grievances in a constructive manner can be extremely difficult. Those who have mastered the method of proper reproof through the application of their study of Torah and mussar can properly perform this mitzva. The following story is told by R' Dovid Hersh Mayer, Menahel of Yeshivas Bais Binyomin in Stamford, Connecticut.

Moshe[26] felt bemused as he entered the wedding hall. Imagine! Here he was, attending the first wedding of a child of one of his *yeshiva* classmates. Decades had passed since then, years that could hardly erase the memories of the times spent together. And now, here they were, gathered together for this special *simcha*.

The rhythmic beat of the lively wedding music shook Moshe out of his reverie. Smiling now, he stood to one side before he joined the dancing, watching as his old classmates danced together, graying beards covering the young faces of the past. It was a beautiful wedding, warm and lively. Moshe felt ready to embrace the entire world.

Then he saw Berel.

The Berel of today was a distinguished, well-respected *talmid chacham* with a noted career in rabbinic service. But as Moshe looked at him, he saw the Berel of the past: Berel the Bully, who had made Moshe his scapegoat throughout their *yeshiva* years. It was Moshe who Berel taunted, Moshe who

---

[26] *All names are fictitious.*

Berel fought, Moshe who was the brunt of all of Berel's practical jokes.

Now, watching Berel standing there in his elegant rabbinic garb, Moshe realized that he had to speak to Berel. The emotional wounds still festered. It was high time they were healed.

Before he could lose his courage, Moshe approached his former classmate. Berel was busily engaged in conversation with another man, so Moshe waited a few polite feet away. The conversation continued for a while, and though Berel did take a moment to galnce at Moshe, he continued to ignore his presence.

Finally, the man walked away. With a slight smile, Berel held out his hand. "*Sholom aleichem*, Reb Moshe," he said politely. "How wonderful to see you after all these years!"

"Wonderful," Moshe replied neutrally.

"Is there something you wanted to speak to me about?"

Moshe took a deep breath. "Yes," he said. "I wanted to tell you that I have something in my possession that I'm sure is very precious to you."

"Oh, really?" Berel raised his eyebrows, looking amused. "What's that?"

Moshe looked at him levelly. "I have your entire future in the World to Come in my pocket," he said.

Berel's look of amusement vanished. "I — I'm not sure I understand," he stammered. "What...?"

Moshe explained. "Reb Berel, when I saw you here tonight, I couldn't help but remember our days together in the *yeshiva*."

Berel flushed. It was evident that he, too, remembered his behavior in those days long past.

"I remember how you used to tease me and belittle me in front of the other boys." Moshe paused. It wasn't easy for him to bring up a matter that had lain dormant for so many years.

"I'm sorry, Moshe," Berel said quickly into Moshe's hesitation. "I hope that you've forgiven me after all these years."

Moshe shook his head. "Well, that's the point, I'm afraid. The incidents that took place back then affected me very deeply. I haven't forgotten them. You can be sure, too, that Hashem has not forgotten them, either."

Berel tried to speak, but Moshe shook his head again. "I'm sure you know, Berel, that the *Chovos Halevovos* states that when a person sins against another, he forfeits all his *mitzvos* to the person he hurt. So you see, in a very real way, I have your *Olam Habaah* in my pocket."

Berel had turned pale by now. "Is it possible to ask you forgiveness?" he asked hoarsely.

Moshe waited a moment before he replied. "It's not that simple," he finally said. "I can't grant you forgiveness if I don't really mean it. Over the years, I have tried many times to forgive and forget all the events of our *yeshiva* years. I tried to tell myself that 'boys will be boys,' and some are simply more aggressive than others. But it hasn't worked. So far, I have not been able to truly forgive you in my heart."

Berel covered his eyes with one hand. "What do you suggest?" he asked, his voice close to a whisper.

Moshe sighed. "I'll do my best to think it through again. Please call me in two weeks or so, and I'll see if I can forgive you." He gave Berel his phone number, then turned and hurried away. He was careful to remain far away from his former classmate for the remainder of the wedding.

Two weeks later, Moshe's telephone rang. Berel was on the line. "Moshe, can you accept my apology now?"

Moshe replied candidly, "Berel, I've thought a great deal about this over the last two weeks. I know I've been able to slightly alter my ill-feelings towards you..."

Berel sighed with relief. "*Baruch Hashem* for that! In that case..."

"However," Moshe interrupted, "I don't think I am able to truly forgive you yet. Please give me another week to think about it. Maybe I'll be able to forgive you by then."

A week later, Berel called Moshe once more. This time, before Moshe could say anything, Berel said, "During the last week, I have mentally reviewed our years together back in *yeshiva*. I have thought about all the times that I wronged you. I know now how terrible it was and I am truly sorry for everything I did." Berel's voice was clearly pleading by now. "Please, Moshe. I beg you. Please accept my apology and forgive me."

"I, too, have spent this past week in thought," Moshe replied. "I realize that you are now truly sorry for the way you treated me. Therefore, Reb Berel, I am happy to say that I can now forgive you completely and wholeheartedly."

"*Baruch Hashem!* Thank you, Reb Moshe, thank you!" Berel was jubilant. "I must tell you that these last three weeks since the wedding have been real torture for me. My entire eternity hung in the balance for the pranks I played as a young boy. Now you have given me back my *Olam Habaah*. Thank you, Reb Moshe. I can finally breathe easily again."

Moshe hung up the phone, smiling to himself. A few gentle words of *mussar* had healed a decades-long wound.

I Was So Sure...

While the mitzva of judging others favorably is never easy, it is most difficult when circumstantial facts seem to point inexorably in one direction. Nevertheless, it is praiseworthy to give one's friend the benefit of the doubt.

The following story, offers ample proof that circumstantial evidence cannot prevent a Jew from being dan lekaf zechus.

R' Nochum[27] hung up the phone and hurried into the kitchen to share the good news with his wife. "That was my old friend, Yossi," he said excitedly. "Guess what? He's a *chosson!*"

R' Nochum's wife smiled. "*Mazel tov!* That's wonderful news. When are they planning to have the wedding?"

"Sometime in December, *b'ezras Hashem*," R' Nochum told her. "This is really exciting. I can't wait to dance at Yossi's *chasunah!*"

"It is exciting," his wife agreed. Then her face clouded. "I'm not so sure we'll be able to attend, though."

"What?" R' Nochum looked blank. "Not go to my old *chavrusa's* wedding? Why ever not?"

His wife sighed. "I'm *im yirtzeh Hashem* expecting the baby in December, remember?"

R' Nochum opened his mouth, then closed it. "You're right," he said sheepishly. "I guess it went clear out of my head." He frowned. "So what do we do now?"

"We'll just have to wait and see," his wife said reasonably. "Maybe we'll be able to work it out somehow."

Months passed. The day of the wedding — and R' Nochum's wife's due date — drew closer. After much discussion of timing and logistics, the two decided that R' Nochum would go the *chasunah* on his own. He would pay a short visit to his parents, who lived in the same area of the *chasunah* hall, and return home late that same night.

---

[27] *Names are fictitious.*

The day of the wedding arrived. R' Nochum rented a car for the two hour drive and set off under a threatening gray sky. Half an hour into the trip, snow flurries began to swirl against the windshield. R' Nochum frowned worriedly as he switched on the windshield wipers. This was not the right kind of weather for a two hour drive, especially when it meant leaving his wife home alone in her condition.

"I'll just have to cut things short," he said aloud as the snow grew heavier. "I can't risk not being able to get home tonight."

He drove straight to his parent's apartment, parking behind a truck that he recognized as belonging to one of the other tenants in the building. He bent his head to the swirling snowflakes and ran into the apartment building as quickly as he could.

After a short, pleasant visit, R' Nochum called home to reassure his wife that he'd arrived safely and to reassure himself that she was fine. Then he bade his parents a warm goodbye and hurried out to the rented car. It now stood alone at the curb. The truck that had been parked right in front of it was gone.

As R' Nochum quickly walked down towards the sidewalk, fumbling in his pocket for the keys, he suddenly stopped short. The front fender looked... Oh, no! Was it really true?

He dashed around to the passenger side of the rented car to double check. Sure enough, there was a bad dent in the fender. What was he going to do now?

As he stood there in the snow, studying the damage, he realized that faint tire tracks led right to the damaged bumper, then swerved out toward the street. R' Nochum pursed his lips. It seemed obvious that his parents' neighbor had accidently backed his truck into the rented car. Sighing, R'

Nochum got into the car and switched on the ignition. He didn't have time to go confront the neighbor now. He'd have to call him from the wedding hall.

R' Nochum arrived at the wedding hall and went straight inside to embrace his former *chavrusa*. He danced for several minutes, then slipped outside into the lobby and hurried over to the pay phone. He called his parents and got the neighbor's phone number, then dialled the new number.

"Hello?" came the voice over the telephone.

"Mr. Lieberman? This is Nochum Hirsch. I was just visiting my parents now, and I parked my car behind your truck." R' Nochum held his breath, wondering what the neighbor would say.

"Yes?" Mr. Lieberman said politely. "What about it?"

R' Nochum had hoped that the man would take the hint, but apparently not. "When I went back outside," he said, choosing his words carefully and making sure to speak in a non-accusatory tone, "I found the left front corner of the car badly dented. There was a tire track in the snow leading right to the car. Ah, would you by any chance know anything about —"

Mr. Lieberman didn't give R' Nochum a chance to finish. "Are you accusing me?" he demanded angrily. "How dare you! I had nothing to do with it!" Without another word, the man slammed the phone down, leaving R' Nochum listening to nothing but the brassy dial tone.

With a resigned sigh, R' Nochum hung up the phone. There was nothing he could do about it. "I might as well enjoy the wedding," he mumbled to himself. "I'll have plenty of time to worry about this later."

After another half hour of dancing, R' Nochum wished Yossi one last *"mazel tov"* before going outside for the cold, two hour drive home. He avoided mentioning anything about the incident to his wife, resolving merely to report to the rental agency in the morning.

The next morning, R' Nochum drove the rented car back to the agency and parked in the lot. Then he took the keys inside to the agent.

"There's a problem, I'm afraid," he said apologetically. "I had the car parked near the curb and someone banged into me rather badly. There's a large dent in the front fender." He suppressed the impulse to give them Mr. Lieberman's name and merely added, "I'm very sorry, but I wasn't able to locate the other party."

"Well, let's go take a look..." The agent went outside, followed by R' Nochum. The man took one short look, then smiled and shook his head. "Nothing to worry about, sir. You didn't put that dent there."

"I didn't?" R' Nochum said, surprised.

"No, sir. That dent was there before you rented the car. I remember when the last person brought the car in. It shouldn't have been rented out before it was fixed, but you didn't put it there, sir. Don't worry about it."

R' Nochum numbly thanked the agent, then slowly walked away, his mind full of self-recrimination. Mr. Lieberman had been right; he really hadn't done anything to the rented car. Despite the "obvious" evidence of the tire track and his apparently guilty reaction on the phone, Mr. Lieberman was innocent, after all.

"I'll have to apologize," R' Nochum said softly. "I should have judged him favorably."

Dan lekaf zechus. One never knows when circumstantial evidence is nothing but circumstance.

Family Ties

R' Tzvi Fishman peered through his windshield. A man was standing on the quiet Monsey street, waving excitedly at his car. What could he possibly want? Puzzled, R' Tzvi pulled his car over to the side and rolled down the window.

"Do you have a phone?" the man asked him.

"No, but I'm going to my mother–in–law's house, and I can use the phone there. Why, what's the problem?"

The man pointed up the street. "There's a man lying on the road over there. I don't know if he's alive or not. Could you call Hatzalah?"

"Sure, my mother–in–law's house is right around the corner. I'll call from there."

R' Tzvi arrived at his mother–in–law's house and immediately went to the phone. "Hatzalah? There's someone lying in the street ... " R' Tzvi gave directions, then hung up the phone.

A short while later, R' Tzvi remembered that there was an important errand he needed to do. "I'll be right back," he told his mother–in–law.

R' Tzvi sat down in the driver's seat and started the car. Unexpectedly, he began to feel lightheaded and woozy. "That's funny," he murmured. Frowning, he shook his head and put the car in gear. But he was disoriented enough to forget to turn on the headlights.

R' Tzvi turned the corner, followed by an officer in a police car, who had noticed that his lights weren't on. Abruptly, the strange feeling in his head became worse. The world began to spin, R' Tzvi blacked out and his car crashed into a telephone pole.

The crash caught everyone's attention. The policeman

slammed on his brakes. Neighbors peeked out the window. And a Hatzalah member who was standing nearby ran over to see what was happening.

The Hatzalah member happened to know R' Tzvi, and he recognized his car. He immediately ran over to the driver's side to see what had happened. His observation led him to suspect the worst: R' Tzvi had suffered a stroke.

The policeman, too, had left his car. The Hatzalah man quickly went over to him.

"We were here because someone had called us about a man lying on the street. It turns out that man is drunk and there's no need for our services. This man in the car, on the other hand, has had a stroke. Why don't you take the drunkard, while we take this other man to the hospital?"

The policeman agreed to the scheme, and R' Tzvi was quickly rushed to the hospital. Fortunately, he arrived in time, and with Hashem's help, he recovered.

After his condition was stabilized, the Hatzalah member came to visit him.

"You know, I called you myself," R' Tzvi told him. "I called my own Hatzalah call!"

What is he talking about? the Haztalah member wondered. He concluded that R' Tzvi was still disoriented from everything that had happened.

It wasn't until later that the story came out. It was R' Tzvi who had called Hatzalah from his mother–in–law's house, and it was because of his call that Hatzalah had been right there, in time to take him to the hospital and save his life.

■ ■ ■

R' Tzvi Fishman had been born in Shanghai, China,

where his father, R' Chanoch Henach, had been learning together with the student body of the Mirrer Yeshiva during World War II. Later on, the family settled in America.

R' Tzvi's family had never compromised on Torah and *mitzvos*. R' Tzvi himself had a particularly strong respect for his parents. Even after his father passed away, R' Tzvi always adhered to his father's customs and practices. He would occasionally admonish other people for accepting customs that their fathers had never practiced, asking them, "Did your father do this?"

On the night after the fast of *Tisha B'Av*, 5755 (1995), R' Tzvi suddenly collapsed. Again, Hatzalah tried to revive him, but this time their efforts failed. Shortly after he was brought to the hospital, R' Tzvi passed away.

The family was devastated. But practical matters kept them from dwelling on their grief. Arrangements had to be made for burial, and R' Tzvi had not given his family any instructions about where he wished to be buried. The family didn't even know where to start.

"Let's try Mr. Rand[28]," Mrs. Fishman suggested.

"Why him?" a family member asked.

Mrs. Fishman shrugged. "I don't know. But he knew him well. Maybe he'll have some ideas."

No one had any other suggestions. So Mr. Rand was called and given the sorrowful news.

"Is there any way you can help us?" the family member asked.

Mr. Rand was taken aback. "I honestly don't know where to begin. But I'll be happy to help you, if I can."

"Well, do you know anything about the Tiferes

---

[28] *Name is fictitious*

Yerushalayim division of the Cyprus Hill Cemetery in Long Island? R' Tzvi's father and grandfather are buried there. If there's room there, that would be a good solution."

"I don't know anything about it myself, but I'll make some calls and get back to you."

After several phone calls, Mr. Rand got the answer. That section was completely filled; indeed, it had been for years.

But there was another section in the same cemetery: the Brisker Division. Perhaps there was room there? Mr. Rand made some more calls, eventually speaking to the director of the Brisker division.

"Look, I have the map in my Long Island office. Perhaps we can meet there and check it out."

"Perfect," Mr. Rand said. "I actually have an appointment in Long Island anyway. This should work out fine."

At the crack of dawn, Mr. Rand drove to Long Island. In the meantime, the family made arrangements for the funeral, though they still didn't know where the burial would be.

Mr. Rand met the director and then glanced at the map. His gaze wandered over the Brisker section. Abruptly, he decided to check out the Tifereth Jerusalem section one last time.

He took the phone and called the curator of that section.

"Are you sure there's nothing at all left there?" he asked. "Could you check the map for me?"

"No, I'm sure it's been filled long ago."

"Just check the map," he urged.

He waited for a minute while the man at the other end shuffled through a few maps. Finally, he came back on.

"You're not going to believe this. I think there actually is one spot available."

"Really?" Mr. Rand was excited. "I'm coming over to take a look."

When he arrived at the cemetery, the curator brought him over to the spot. A marking nearby indicated that the plot had once been used by someone named Chaim Ledkansky[29], though it was available now.

Mr. Rand called the secretary of the Tiferes Yerushalayim section. "I've been told that there is one space available."

"As far as I know, every spot is taken," the man replied. "It's been filled for years."

"This spot was used by Chaim Ladkansky, but it's open now."

"Oh, I see." The man sounded uneasy. "I really don't know what to tell you. But you're welcome to check into it. I'll give you the number of someone to call."

Mr. Rand set to work. It took a few phone calls, but eventually everything was sorted out. The plot was available, and Mr. Rand called the family with the news.

"Bring the *aron* to the Tiferes Yerushalyim section. I managed to get a place there."

As the burial proceeded, the family was astonished to discover that the plot arranged for R' Tzvi was right next to that of his father and grandfather!

POSTSCRIPT:

After the funeral was over, Mr. Rand called Rabbi Ledkansky, Chaim's father. "Would you mind telling me more about your son?" he asked.

"My son Chaim passed away in 1956, when we were living in America," Rabbi Ledkansky told him. "Years later, after we moved to Israel, someone came over to me. He told me that he had known my son as a young boy, and my son

---

[29] *Name is fictitious.*

had told him once that when he dies, he would like to be buried in Israel.

"At the time my son made that comment, he was young and perfectly healthy. That he had made such an unusual and unexpected statement when he was healthy really preyed on my mind. So eventually, in the early seventies, I had him transferred to Israel."

4

TORAH AND MITZVOS

A Priceless Gift

Shabbos Radiance

Chanuka Miracle

The Angel's Shofar

Mitzvah Connection

Sagacious Attire

Guiding Light

Holy Counsel

The Right Choice

A Close Cut

Of Bagels and Locks

Not for Nothing

The Father He Never Knew

4
Torah and Mitzvos

A Priceless Gift[30]

"Mazel tov, mazel tov!"

Shaul Peirletzky[31] smiled as he greeted family and friends. Years of preparation and study had preceeded this special night, and he was delighted that so many had come to share in his *simcha*.

Shaul was celebrating his completion of *Shas*. Reaching this point had not been easy. There had been many times over the years that his learning had been in jeopardy. But Shaul had persevered, and now he was justifiably proud of his accomplishment.

Shaul rose from his seat, standing at the front of the

---

[30] The following story was related by Rabbi Mordechai Shain.
[31] Name is fictitious

room. A hush fell over the crowd as he began to speak.

"Years ago, I left *yeshiva*, got married and went to work for a living. The change from my *yeshiva* days, when I was immersed in Torah learning, to a working environment, where I hardly learned Torah, was abrupt and difficult, and I couldn't help feeling empty and unfulfilled.

"One night, I had a sobering dream. I was an elderly man living in an old–age home. Fortunately, it was a *frum* home, filled with many people who were learning *gemara* and utilizing their last years for Torah study. But I had lost my inspiration for learning years before, and I was unable to even look at a *sefer*. Time hung heavy on my hands.

"At lunch time, one of the learned residents gave a *gemara* lecture. Many of those attending were very attentive, and they were involved in the class. But I simply couldn't get into the learning. I ended up falling asleep with my head on the table.

"One gentleman began going around during the class, pouring out cups of tea. As he neared me, he accidently tripped and spilled some hot tea on my neck.

"I jumped up and yelled so loud that I woke myself up!

"Well, the dream was over. As I sat there, bathed in sweat, I realized that it had only been a dream. But how likely was it to come true? At that moment, I decided that I would never become the old man in my dream, sleeping during a *gemara* class. Somehow, I would make time for Torah learning.

"The very next morning I joined a *gemara* class. It was hard at first, but with resolve and perseverance, I found that learning became an important part of my day and my life.

"And so tonight I am making this *siyum*, to thank Hashem for giving me this eternal gift. And I hope it will be as much an inspiration for others as it is for me."

Shabbos Radiance

R' Yosef Yitzchok Parnes was born on the thirteenth day of Teves 5635 (1875). He was the firstborn son of R' Avrohom Yehosua Parnes and his wife, Temme. As he grew up, Yosef Yitzchok's devotion to Torah was only matched by his *yiras shomayim* and love of Hashem.

R' Yosef Yitzchok's family was originally very wealthy. His father was a *talmid chacham* and a generous *baal tzedakah*. But after R' Yosef Yitzchok married and had eight children, their financial status took a turn for the worse. The poverty-stricken father was advised by his *rebbe*, Reb Moishele Drombrover, to take his family to the United States.

R' Yosef Yitzchok arrived in America in 1907, and his family joined him a short time later. They initially settled on the Lower East Side.

During those early years in America, R' Yosef Yitzchok found it very hard to earn a living. There was no money to pay the rent, and eventually, his entire family was thrown out of their apartment. With no other options, R' Yosef Yitzchok moved into the cellar of the *shul* where he *davened*.

One day, a man who had *yahrzeit* came to *daven* in the *shul*. He happened to go down to the cellar, and he noticed children running around.

"What's going on here?" he asked the *shammas*.

The *shammas* pointed to R' Yosef Yitzchok, who was standing in a corner, looking into a *sefer*.

"You see that man learning over there? Those are his children. They've been living in the cellar for a few weeks because he was evicted from his apartment."

The man was moved by R' Yosef Yitzchok's plight. He walked over to where R' Yosef Yitzchok was learning.

"Reb Yid, I see your family had to move into the dark cellar, among the oven and the coal. I can't bear to see such a sight. Please, go find an apartment. I'll give you the rent for a few months."

"I see you haven't *davened* yet," R' Yosef Yitzchok replied. "First *daven*, and then I'll give you an answer."

The man was puzzled. What was there to think about before accepting such an offer? Nevertheless, he went to *daven*.

In the meantime, R' Yosef Yitzchok made some inquiries about the man. "Is he *shomer Shabbos*?" he asked.

"No," he was told. "That man's business is open on *Shabbos*."

When *davening* was over, the man again approached R' Yosef Yitzchok. "Nu, what do you say?"

"Thank you very much for your good intentions, but you really can't help me."

The man was taken aback. "What do you mean, I can't help you? How do you know?"

"You see," R' Yosef Yitzchok explained, "I have a principle not to use any money that was earned on the holy *Shabbos* day. I hear that your business is open on *Shabbos*, so you cannot help me."

"I simply can't understand that," the man said. "You may want to be *frum* for yourself, but how can you be so cruel to your children?"

Upset and bewildered, the man left.

When the man came home, his wife greeted him.

"Listen," he told her. "You won't believe this story."

He described R' Yosef Yitzchok's poverty, then went on to relate how R' Yosef Yitzchok had refused his generous offer.

"Really? I have to see this."

The woman went along with her husband at *mincha* time,

and she went down to the cellar. As she descended the steps, a boy also came to the cellar door, holding a bag in his hand.

"What do you have in the bag, my child?" she asked, smiling kindly.

The boy showed her his purchase: pieces of banana from the banana vendor, which had been cut after the spoiled sections were discarded.

The woman went up to R' Yosef Yitzchok.

"My husband wants to help you by giving you money for your rent. Why do you refuse it? How can you stand seeing your wife and children suffer like this?"

"I do not use money that was earned on *Shabbos*," R' Yosef Yitzchok answered simply.

"But the people who are *shomer Shabbos* aren't offering you any money," the woman argued.

"Then we don't need it. If Hashem wants us to have, He will either provide for us directly, or through a *shomer Shabbos* person. Since He does not, it is a sign that we are to live this way."

The woman was moved by R' Yosef Yitzchok's sincere beliefs. She took her husband aside.

"This is a rare opportunity. Why don't we close our business just for this *Shabbos*? That way, the money we earn next week will be kosher, and we can give the money to him."

The man consented. And when R' Yosef Yitzchok was approached, he also agreed to the idea.

That *Shabbos*, the man closed his business, and he gave R' Yosef Yitzchok the money for his rent.

But the story does not end there. The man and his wife kept up their contact with R' Yosef Yitzchok. And as *Chazal* say, "One *mitzva* leads to another." From keeping one *Shabbos* and the *mitzva* of *tzedakkah*, they eventually became *shomrei Shabbos* and complete *baalei teshuva*.

Years later, when R' Yosef Yitzchok passed away, someone returning from his funeral remarked, "Did you see the men wearing *chassideshe* clothing carrying the *aron* on their shoulders for so many blocks? They are the children and grandchildren of that couple who paid the rent."

CHANUKAH MIRACLE[32]

Spring, 1915. The rapid staccato of gunfire, the screams of the wounded, the shouts of advancing soldiers all blended into the unmistakable sound of war.

One German soldier suddenly screamed, his voice joining the general cacaphony. He had been preparing to sprint ahead, but a bullet had found its mark. Instead of advancing, he fell to the ground.

Twenty yards behind him, another soldier crawled along the ground until he reached his wounded comrade. Seizing him by the belt, he slowly dragged him toward a trench at the rear. Medics were waiting with a canvas stretcher, and they carried the wounded man away.

An act of heroism? Perhaps. But such incidents were not unusual in wartime, and it was soon forgotten.

1938: Not a good year for a Jew to be in Germany. Over the past two years, special laws had been passed limiting the Jews' participation in what had been considered a modern,

---

[32] *Published by arrangement with Arnold Geier and the Berkley Publishing Group, based on the author's story as told in* Heroes of the Holocaust, *Berkley Publishing, February 1998.*

civilized country. The conviction that the social and political winds would change, and that persecution belonged to bygone days, had faded. Many Jews had made contact with friends, relatives and organizations, hoping to find someone to sponsor them for emigration to any country that was willing to have them. The list included the United States, China, Columbia, England, Palestine and South Africa. But most Jews did not have friends or relatives abroad, and were resigned to facing their future in Europe with a mix of hope and trepidation.

Arnold Geier's family was more fortunate. His mother's sister and husband had already moved to New York back in the 1920's. His uncle worked as a night janitor in a skyscraper. The family had little money, but they made up for it with an abundance of compassion, love and courage. Arnold's aunt set to work, searching high and low for anyone who had the money and the heart to sponsor Arnold's family, including his aunt and grandparents, for immigration to the United States.

This was no easy task. Sponsoring a family meant preparing an affidavit, consisting of disclosure of income and financial holdings, copies of tax returns, and a sworn guarantee that the sponsor would support the newcomers so they would not become a financial burden to the U.S. Government. So it was no surprise that despite Arnold's aunt's pleas, most people were unwilling to help. Finally, one man, an Orthodox Jewish manufacturer, agreed to sponsor Arnold's family.

In the fall of 1938, the Geier family finally received their affidavits. The mail arrived on a Thursday. Arnold's father, Yehuda Geier, immediately delivered his papers to the U.S. Embassy, and received a quota number for his family. Arnold's grandfather, however, brought his papers to the Embassy the following Monday.

Disaster! The quota had just been filled. The affidavit was not accepted.

November 8, 1938. Arnold's grandparents and his aunt Dora were in their apartment in the Jewish neighborhood of Berlin. A sudden, loud knock on their door froze them in their seats. Knocks like that in Germany in those days usually meant trouble.

No one moved. The knock sounded again. Finally, Arnold's grandfather opened the door.

A tall man with Germanic features was standing on the threshold. The man looked furtively to either side.

"May I come in, please." It was more a command than a request.

Arnold's grandfather quickly stepped aside, and the man entered, closing the door behind him.

"Herr Geier, I can only stay a moment."

The man glanced at him, but then looked away, avoiding Mr. Geier's gaze.

"Herr Geier, do you remember that you once saved a soldier on the battlefield, many years ago?"

Arnold's grandfather blinked in surprise. He had nearly forgotten the incident. But now that the man mentioned it, memories came flooding back.

He nodded cautiously. "Yes, I remember. What of it?"

"I am that soldier. I have never forgotten what you did for me. I work for the Chief of Police in Berlin now, but I've always kept track of you.

"Listen carefully. Tomorrow night, the police and SS will be rounding up Jews from all over Germany. I have seen the list and your name is on it. Do whatever you have to do."

Now the man met his gaze. "My debt to you is paid. *Auf Wiedersehn!*"

With that, he turned, walked through the door and

disappeared into the darkness.

Arnold's grandfather stood still. His mind raced with shock, bewilderment and fear. A moment later, he leaped into action. Grabbing the phone, he called his son Yehuda.

"Yehuda, could you come right over, please?"

"What's wrong?" his son asked in alarm.

The elder Mr. Geier was afraid to mention any details on the phone. "Just come over now, please," he repeated.

Concerned, Yehuda Geier took a taxi over to his father's house. His father quickly told him about the warning he had received. The two of them then sat down and started to think. They needed a plan, and there was no time to waste.

At length they decided on a course of action. For the rest of that night, and most of the next day, both men worked the phones, spreading the news that Mr. *Malach Hamaves* (Angel of Death) would be coming to town that evening. They suggested that he should be greeted by all of their friends, and that news of his arrival should be passed on to others. Hundreds of people were contacted during those twelve hours.

That afternoon, Yehuda Geier told his children that he would be going on a business trip for a few days. Actually, he took public transportation to the home of one of his customers, a self-professed anti-Nazi who had offered to shelter him for a few days. Mr. Geier spent the night of November 9, 1938 by his friend. History would give that night a different name: *Kristallnacht*.

Arnold was twelve years old at the time. It was not unusual for his father to go on a business trip, and he remained blithely unconcerned. But on the morning of November 10, he came in for a rude awakening.

A large hand on his shoulder suddenly shook him out of his sleep. Arnold opened his eyes, and discovered a giant man in a black uniform looming above his head. The silver decorations on the man's tunic glittered in the morning light.

"Where is your father!" he shouted.

Arnold was terrified. He could barely speak.

"He's on a business trip," he managed to say.

The giant let go of his shoulder. He looked under Arnold's bed and in his closet. Grumbling, he left to search the rest of the apartment. Again he came up empty-handed. He angrily confronted Arnold's mother.

"As soon as he gets back, I'll have him call you," Arnold heard his mother say. Finally, the Nazi left.

For the first time, Arnold's ears registered the raucous noises coming from the streets. He went over to his mother. "What's going on?" he asked in fright.

"Shh, don't worry," his mother said soothingly. "Everything will be all right."

Arnold's mother quickly got breakfast together for Arnold and his fifteen year old sister. As the family was eating, the noise level from the street seemed to swell. To the ears of the anxious family came the sounds of breaking glass, shouts, laughter and screams of terror.

The family rushed over to the window, three stories above the street, and gazed down on a scene of terror. Hundreds of men, women and children were milling about, watching helplessly as storm troopers smashed the windows of nearby shops and painted anti–Semitic slogans on the walls. "DIE, JEW! DON'T BUY FROM JEWS! THE JEWS ARE OUR MISFORTUNE!"

Other troopers were beating a bearded elderly Jew with their nightsticks and bare fists. To his horror, Arnold realized that they were trying to pull off the man's beard.

"No, no!" he screamed out the window. "Don't, leave him alone!"

His voice was lost in the general pandemonium below. Arnold watched, sick at heart, as policemen stood nearby and watched, doing nothing to interfere.

Arnold's mother pulled him away from the window. Where is Papa? Arnold wondered to himself, as tears ran down his cheeks.

Where was Yehuda Geier? He had spent the night in his customer's home, hoping that the alarm had been false. But by early morning, the radio had reported a "spontaneous citizen's outburst" against Jews throughout the city and the entire country. The warning had been real.

Now Yehuda needed to come up with a more permanent solution. He didn't feel secure staying with his customer. The man professed to be anti–Nazi, but his feelings might change if he were really put to the test. No, he needed another idea.

What about their affidavits? Yehuda had heard that the Nazis would not bother people who had visas for another country. With their affidavits, they were eligible for U.S. visas. Perhaps the Embassy could do something for them.

The American Embassy did not open before nine o'clock, so Yehudah Geier had to use up at least two hours. He spent the time riding whatever buses and trolleys were still operating, changing from one to another to avoid any suspicion. Finally, as nine o'clock neared, he took the the bus that led into the center of town and past the American Embassy.

As the bus approached the Embassy, Yehuda saw hundreds of people, many of them wearing pajamas and robes, jammed into the area against the front of the Embassy, trying to push open the gates. Several people stood on the other side of the gates, watching what was going on but still keeping the gates closed. Gestapo and SS men were roaming the fringes of the mob, picking up screaming and struggling figures and dragging them to waiting trucks.

The time: twenty minutes before nine.

Yehuda stayed on the bus for exactly ten more minutes. Then he got off, crossed the street, and boarded another bus that would be going back toward the Embassy. If his timing was right, he would end up in front of the Embassy at exactly nine o'clock.

As Yehuda stepped off the bus in front of the Embassy, the gates opened, and a flood of people poured onto the grounds. Yehuda joined the mob and pushed his way in with the others. The SS men and Gestapo were shoved aside, and Yehuda found himself on American soil, safe from German authority.

The Embassy people were sympathetic and did whatever they could. They brought in food and allowed the crowd to sit in hallways, doorways and gardens. They tried to calm the frightened adults and children.

So many people were milling around that Yehuda found it nearly impossible to speak to an Embassy official. After several hours, he finally managed to get someone's attention.

"Look, I have an official visa number," he pleaded with her. "Could you arrange an appointment for me with an officer?"

"Well, I don't know," the young woman said doubtfully. "With all this going on, there isn't too much work getting done. I'll see what I can do."

Yehuda waited hopefully. But the hours passed, and the woman did not return.

Five o'clock: closing time. Hundreds of people still lingered on the grounds, refusing to leave. A high-ranking Embassy official left his office to plead with the crowd. Yehuda saw his chance.

He grabbed the man's sleeve. "Please," he begged, with

tears in his eyes. "I have a visa number. Could you have it changed into a real visa right now?"

The harrassed officer stared at Yehuda, then at the crowd, and then back at Yehuda. He shook his head in disbelief. Finally, he motioned to an assistant.

"Take care of this man now," he directed. "If he checks out, then give him his visa."

Within an hour, Yehuda Geier was the proud owner of a precious American visa. It was no more than a large rubber stamp on one page of his passport, with names and dates of birth inserted. But on that day in Germany, it was life itself.

Yehuda went home. On the way, he was stopped several times. He showed his visa and was left alone.

Yehuda's father, Mr. Geier, had hidden with a German family on the outskirts of the city. He returned only after the pogrom had died down. He still had an unused affadavit, but he never obtained an official number for a visa, because the quota was never reopened. He, his wife, and Yehuda's sister Dora did not survive.

December 25, 1938. The Germans that Yehuda Geier and his family encountered that morning seemed almost mellow, as they celebrated their holiday. The Jewish world, too, was celebrating the last night of Chanuka. And Yehuda Geier had his own private celebration. He and his family were finally on their way out of Germany, headed toward a new life in the United States of America.

The day dawned sunny but chilly. The Geier family was quietly seated in a second–class compartment on a train that had left Berlin early that morning, which was due to arrive in Holland at night. Two stern Germans shared the compartment with Mr. and Mrs. Geier, their fifteen year old daughter, and twelve year old Arnold.

The children peered out the window and occupied themselves with chatter about the sights racing by. Yehuda, their father, remained deep in thought. Mrs. Geier interrupted her reading from time to time to whisper to her husband.

"Don't worry," Arnold once heard her say. "I'm sure that under these circumstances, Hashem will forgive you for not celebrating the last night of Chanuka."

The journey continued uneventfully. The family ate the sandwiches they had prepared. After lunch, they dozed, and then stretched their legs with occasional walks to adjoining cars. They chatted quietly to avoid disturbing the Germans in their compartment. The miles slowly went by.

As darkness settled gently over the countryside, the train slowed. Its brakes squealing and hissing, the train drew into a special railway station on the German–Dutch border and jerked to a stop. This was it: their final encounter with Nazis and the Gestapo. The family braced themselves. Freedom was close at hand. Just a little more time, a few more miles, before they could begin their new lives.

The train sat in the station for an endless ten minutes. The family watched teams of police officers and Gestapo agents getting organized for a thorough examination of the passengers' passports and travel papers. Finally, small groups of officials began to clamber aboard.

Just then, all the lights went out.

The train and the station were completely black. Noises of confusion and alarm cut through the darkness. Several people struck matches, illuminating their pale, frightened faces with a flickering, eerie light. The children held back their screams.

Abruptly, Yehuda Geier stood up. He reached into the luggage rack above the seats, groping around for his overcoat. He pulled the coat down, reached into one of the pockets and pulled out a small packet.

Yehuda walked over to the window. The children watched him fumble with the packet for a moment, then take out a match and a single candle. He struck the match, lit a candle, and then, slowly and deliberately, used its flame to warm the bottoms of eight Chanuka candles, which he then placed neatly in a row on the window ledge. He murmured the appropriate blessings and lit each one carefully. Finally, he placed the ninth candle over to one side.

Yehuda Geier returned slowly to his seat and carefully sat down. For the first time in many long months, he smiled.

A shout came from the platform. "There's a light over there!"

Moments later, several of the police and Gestapo had entered the compartment. One police officer sat down right next to the Chanuka candles.

"We'll check the passports over here," he directed. He turned to Yehuda. "That was really an excellent idea you had, to bring along travel candles. Thank you for helping us out here."

One by one, the passengers brought their papers over to the Chanuka candles to be checked by the German officials. The Geiers retreated from the compartment and watched the amazing scene from the passageway near the door.

The candles burned steadily for half an hour. Then they began to flicker, signalling that there was no more than a few minutes of light left.

As abruptly as they had gone off, the lights came on again. The passengers blinked in the sudden harsh glare, relieved at the disappearance of the flickering shadows. The German officials left the compartment to continue checking papers on the rest of the train. As they made their way into the passageway, one officer turned to Yehuda, thanked him curtly and then walked out.

Yehuda turned to his son and smiled. "Remember this moment," he said softly. "For just as in the days of the Macabees, a great miracle happened here."

THE ANGEL'S SHOFAR

When Rabbi Zalman Friedman was a young boy, he and his family lived in an apartment building in Boro Park. Mrs. Klein, an elderly holocaust survivor, lived just below them. Mrs. Klein had gone through a lot in her life, but her commitment to Hashem's *mitzvos* had remained firm, and she was always careful to fulfill each *mitzva* in the best possible manner. Even now that she was aged and frail, she made a point of going to *shul* every *Shabbos*, where she poured out her heart to Hashem.

Mrs. Klein had a special attachment to one specific *mitzva*: hearing the *shofar* on *Rosh Hashanah*. This *mitzva* hadn't always been easy for her to fulfill, and Mrs. Klein had many stories of the times she had nevertheless managed to hear the *shofar*, despite the self–sacrifice it involved.

Zalman would often watch his elderly neighbor make her way to *shul* on *Shabbos*. Beset by ill health, with her strength ebbing, Mrs. Klein would determinedly take each slow step to *shul*, until she finally reached her destination.

Rosh Hashana had arrived. Mrs. Klein woke up early *yom tov* morning, planning as always to go to *shul* to hear the *shofar*. But when she tried to get out of bed, she was shocked to discover that her legs were too weak to support her.

"What's happening to me?" she whispered, frightened.

Again she tried to get up. But each time she stood, she

lost her balance and fell back into her bed. She was unable to take a single step.

For this to happen on *Rosh Hashana* morning, of all times! How would she ever get to hear the *shofar*? Bursting into tears, Mrs. Klein poured her sorrow into her prayers. "Please," she begged Hashem. "Give me just a bit of strength, so I can get up and go to *shul* to hear the *shofar*."

Feeling drained after her impassioned plea, Mrs. Klein calmed down somewhat. She *davened* the morning prayers, and then reached for her *tehillim*. As she spoke the ancient words, pouring out her heart in prayer, once again she asked Hashem to give her strength.

All at once, the quiet of her apartment was interrupted by the piercing sound of a *shofar*. Mrs. Klein jerked upright in amazement. Was she dreaming? No, the sound came again. The *shofar* was being blown in the correct order, just as she would be hearing it if she had been in *shul*.

Tears streaming down her cheeks, Mrs. Klein opened her *machzor* and followed along. "Who could be blowing the *shofar*?" she marveled. "It must be an angel from heaven!"

Zalman's mother used to go downstairs to visit her elderly neighbor every *Shabbos*. On the *Shabbos* after Rosh Hashana, Mrs. Klein excitedly told her about the angel who had blown the *shofar* for her on *yom tov*. "Look at the special gift Hashem gave me," Mrs. Klein said, tears of happiness in her eyes.

"Well," Mrs. Friedman said with a smile, "how would you like to meet that angel?"

Mrs. Klein looked at her in surprise. "What do you mean?"

"Your angel happens to be my son, Zalman. A while ago, Zalman was visiting a cousin who had a nice *shofar* collection. When he noticed Zalman's interest in the *shofros*, he offered him one as a gift, and even taught him how to blow it.

"Zalman was delighted with his *shofar*. He practiced over and over, until he learned how to blow perfectly. Since then, every year on Rosh Hashana, Zalman comes home after *davening* and blows all the sounds on the *shofar*."

The following day, when Mrs. Klein was completely recovered, she visited the Friedman's and presented Zalman with a gift.

"Thank you for making my Rosh Hashana so special. You probably don't realize what you did for me. But as far as I'm concerned, you were a messenger from Hashem."

Who could have imagined, Zalman mused, that such a great *mitzva* would come out of such a simple deed?

Mitzva Connection

The Mishnah states, "One mitzva leads to another mitzva." (Avos 4:2) When a person does a mitzva, the deed is not done and forgotten; on the contrary, one can expect other mitzvos to follow in its wake.

R' Mordche Katz[33] often travelled to other cities. Once, on a trip in the southern United States, the local *rav*, Rabbi Gold, approached him and asked him if he would be willing to give a lecture on the basics of *Chumash* and *Rashi*. R' Mordche, who was always willing to be *marbitz Torah* in any

---

[33] *All names are fictitious.*

way possible, readily agreed.

The *shiur* was attended by a number of *baalei batim*. After the lecture, one of the participants approached R' Mordche with a diffident smile.

"My name's Ira Schwartz," the man introduced himself. "I just wanted to tell you, Rabbi, how much I enjoyed your lecture. You really have a way of making complicated things seem simple."

"Thank you," R' Mordche replied warmly. "I'm glad you enjoyed the *shiur*."

Mr. Schwartz hesitated a moment, then added, "I guess it's sort of pretentious of me to even suggest it, but — well, do you think I would be able to learn together with you, for as long as you're here in town?"

R' Mordche was slightly taken aback, but he readily agreed. "I'm always available for a Jew who wants to learn Torah," he assured Mr. Schwartz. The two of them learned together each night for the next week until it was time for R' Mordche to return to New York.

"I really appreciate your learning with me, Rabbi Katz," Ira said sincerely. "I really feel I got a lot out of our sessions."

"It was a pleasure," R' Mordche assured him again. The two said warm goodbyes, and R' Mordche left for the airport for his flight back home.

A year later, the phone rang in the Katz's home. R' Mordche's wife picked up the receiver, listened for a moment, then held the phone out to her husband. "It's for you," she said.

R' Mordche took the phone. "Hello?"

"Rabbi Katz?" said a vaguely familiar voice. "This is Ira Schwartz. I don't know if you remember me..."

"Of course I do!" R' Mordche exclaimed as his mind flashed back to his Southern trip of last year. "We learned together for a week, and you drove me to the airport. Are you in New York now?"

"No, I'm back home now." Mr. Schwartz sounded pleased to be remembered. "I had a real tough time tracking you down, Rabbi Katz. I was in New York a little while ago, but I didn't have your number."

"So how did you find my number now?" R' Mordche asked curiously.

"Well, when I got back home, the rabbi of our *shul* — do you remember Rabbi Gold? — was making a *bris*. The *mohel* was from New York. After the ceremony, one of the other men in *shul* mentioned to me that the *mohel* was the brother of the rabbi I'd learned with last year. So I went over to the *mohel*, and sure enough, he was your brother. I asked him for your phone number, and that's how I got in touch with you now."

"Well, Ira," R' Mordche said cheerfully, "if you went to all that trouble to get my phone number, there must be something I can do for you."

"I certainly hope so," Ira said, his voice suddenly turning sober.

"Hashem helped you contact me," R' Mordche said soothingly. "I'm sure I'll be able to help you. What's troubling you?"

There was a moment of silence, then a sigh came down the line. "It's my children, Rabbi Katz," Ira said sadly. "They're growing up now, and I don't like the way they're turning out. There's no Hebrew day school here, you know, and I send them to public school. They learn from their non-Jewish friends, and they're going from bad to worse. I must get them out of the public school system before it's too late, but what other choice do I have?"

"It's certainly a serious problem," R' Mordche said slowly. "Let's discuss your different options..."

The two men remained on the phone in deep, earnest conversation for a long time. The final outcome? The Schwartz family packed their bags and resettled in New York, where the Schwartz boys were able to attend good *yeshivos*.

Mr. Schwartz, delighted with the turn of events, remained in close contact with R' Mordche, whose willingness to spend a few hours in Torah study with a layman from a small Southern town had resulted in a family's deeper commitment to Torah values and Torah education. When R' Mordche mentioned one day that he needed to go back to Ira's old home town, Ira immediately offered him the keys to his old house.

"We never sold it," Ira explained. "We've had tenants living there off and on over the years, but it's empty now. Save yourself the price of a hotel, Rabbi Katz. I'd consider it an honor."

R' Mordche thanked Ira for his generosity and accepted the offer. The house was centrally located and made things much easier for R' Mordche during his stay.

One morning after *shul*, a respectable looking businessman offered to drive R' Mordche back to the house. The two men settled into the front seat of the expensive, air conditioned car and set off.

"I appreciate the ride," R' Mordche remarked as they drove out of the *shul's* parking lot.

"My pleasure, Rabbi," the man assured him. "My name's Harry Goldsmith, by the way."

They drove in silence for a few moments. Then, as they stopped by a red light, Harry turned to R' Mordche. "Rabbi, do you think you can give me some advice?"

R' Mordche was a little surprised that Mr. Goldsmith would want advice from a stranger, but he said willingly enough, "If I can be of any help to you Harry,

I'll certainly try my best."

"Thank you." The light turned green, and Harry pressed on the accelerator. He concentrated on his driving and said without looking at R' Mordche, "You know, Rabbi, I wasn't always a religious man."

"Really?" R' Mordche looked at Harry with surprise. He seemed to be the typical religious businessman.

"No, I wasn't. I've only been religious for a couple of years now. I'd like to tell you how it happened."

"Go ahead," R' Mordche said encouragingly.

"I'd been laid off work for a long time, and I was getting more and more depressed," Harry began. "The worse things got, the more desperate I felt. I used to sit and drink away my troubles in the local bar — not that it helped me very much.

"One day, as I was sitting and staring into my whiskey, two well dressed businessmen entered the bar. I was the only one there, so they came over to me and asked me if I would be willing to help them out a little.

"I wasn't entirely sober, but I asked them what they wanted. They explained that they had just negotiated a major business deal and they needed an unaffiliated party to act as go between. They wanted to know if I would be interested in acting as broker for their business deal.

"They didn't go into much detail. As I said, I wasn't really sure what they were getting at, but I asked, 'What's in it for me?' When they promised to give me five percent of the deal, I agreed. I mean, what did I have to lose? I signed my name on a few papers and they handed me a check. They left the bar, and I stuffed the check into my pocket and went back to my whiskey."

"So what happened?" R' Mordche asked, spellbound.

Harry smiled. "Well, I finally found my way back home.

I'd almost forgotten about the whole incident, but when I dug my keys out of the pocket, my fingers touched the check. I went inside and handed the check to my wife.

"I still hadn't actually looked at the check, you understand. So when my wife gave this shriek, I looked at her like she was crazy.

" 'What's wrong with you?' I demanded.

" 'Where did you get this check?' she gasped.

" 'I did a little deal in the bar tonight. Why, what's wrong?' "

"She tried once or twice to say something, but she couldn't get her voice to work. Finally, she just held the check up so I could read it. I looked at it, squeezed my eyes shut, and looked at it again. I pinched myself. I shook my head violently. But no matter what I did, that check remained the same.

"Rabbi, that check was for seven hundred thousand dollars!"

"And was it a good check?" R' Mordche asked.

Harry chuckled. "That's just what I asked my wife that night. We had no idea if the men who gave me the check really had that kind of money. But we figured it wouldn't hurt to try, so we deposited the check in our banking account and spent the next several days chewing our fingernails while we waited to see if the check cleared. Sure enough, we finally got word from the bank. The check had cleared! We were rich!"

"So what happened next?" R' Mordche urged as Harry stopped to catch his breath.

"Well, my wife and I sat down that night and had a good, long talk. I mean, this was obviously a gift sent to us from Heaven. Two men walk into a bar and give a total stranger a five percent cut of a deal worth millions of dollars? This had to be straight from G–d. We both agreed to that, but how could we go about thanking G–d for what He'd done for us? Finally, my wife said that she'd read once that G–d wants His people to follow His will. We decided that we must start to obey G–d's will by living as observant Jews. The next day, we got in contact with Rabbi Gold. Within a few months, we were fully committed."

Harry fell silent. R' Mordche waited a moment to see if he would continue, then ventured, "Your story is an amazing example of Divine Providence, Harry. I don't quite see where you need my help."

Harry sighed. "Well, you see, Rabbi, I get the feeling that I'm running into trouble. With the money, we bought a fancy house and this car." He gestured at the plush leather seats. "I've made some investments, too, hoping to increase my capital, but they've all failed. I'm beginning to be afraid that I'm eating up all my money, Rabbi." He paused. "I don't want to go back to where I was."

R' Mordche sat quietly for a few moments, arranging his thoughts. Then he looked up. "Let me tell you a parable," he suggested.

"There was once a man who wanted to do something different during his life, something that everyone else would talk about. He thought about it for a while, then decided to make a solo trip across the Atlantic Ocean. He purchased a boat and stocked up on all necessary provisions, including fuel.

"As he was about to set sail, he thought he could get some extra attention if he blew a few smoke signals. After all, the whole purpose of his trip was to attract other people's attention. Wouldn't this be the best way to start?

"So the man blew a few signals. People noticed and began to gather around to watch. The man enjoyed the attention so much that he kept blowing smoke signals, until the entire pier was crowded with people watching and pointing at him.

"Finally, the man decided it was time to embark on his voyage. But when he tried to start the motor, the boat wouldn't budge. He had used up all his fuel, blowing smoke signals!"

R' Mordche completed the story and looked steadily at Harry. "You see, Harry, it works the same way with us. Let's say a man needs fifty thousand dollars a year to live on, and Hashem gives him half a million dollars for the next ten years. The man doesn't realize that the money is meant to last a decade, and he frivolously spends it all in the first year or two. He buys unnecessary luxuries and spends money like water. What he's really doing is blowing smoke signals to show off; and when he finds that he doesn't have enough money, he turns to Hashem in anguish and asks, `Where is my sustenance for this year?' Can't you just hear the answer, Harry? 'Sorry, but you blew it!' "

As R' Mordche finished his explanation, Harry turned his head and spent several minutes staring out the car window. Then he turned back to R' Mordche, a shy, awkward smile on his face.

"You're right, Rabbi," he said quietly. "I guess I have been 'blowing smoke signals' instead of using the money properly. I think I've got the right outlook now."

"I'm sure you'll be fine, Harry," R' Mordche told him. "I'd better be going now." He opened the car door. "Thank you for the ride, Harry. I'm leaving town in a few days, but please keep in touch."

Harry did, indeed, keep in touch with R' Mordche. Every Friday morning, he still calls R' Mordche to tell him news of his family and the community and to wish him a "Good *Shabbos.*"

The initial *mitzva* that R' Mordche did by agreeing to

give a single *shiur* in a small Southern town had reaped enormous benefits and helped bring two Jewish families closer to *Yiddishkeit*.

SAGACIOUS ATTIRE

Rabbi Zalman Friedman, now a member of Beth Medrash Govoha in Lakewood, N.J.,[34] spent several years learning in the Mirrer Yeshiva in Yerushalayim. During that time he would travel periodically to Bnei Brak, where he could bask in the radiance of the Steipler Gaon, *zt"l*, HaRav Yaakov Yisroel Kanievsky (1889–1985).

One year, after spending Yom Kippur in Bnei Brak, R' Zalman decided to make one last stop at the Steipler's house. He wanted to purchase a few of the *tzaddik's sefarim* and, at the same time, ask for his blessing before his return to the States.

It was about an hour and a half after *davening* had ended when R' Zalman arrived at the Steipler's home. When he entered, he found the Steipler seated behind his desk, still wearing his *Shabbos* clothing and *kittel*, reciting *Tehillim* and oblivious to everything around him.

R' Zalman carefully approached the desk and handed the Steipler his request, written on a piece of paper.[35] In the note, R' Zalman explained that he was from America and that

---

[34] *Author of sefer* Lehodos U'lehalel

[35] *This was the common practice in the Steipler's later years, when it became hard for him to hear.*

he would shortly be returning to the States. He asked to purchase a few detailed *sefarim* and to receive the Steipler's blessing.

The Steipler read the note. He looked up at R' Zalman.

"I'm afraid I can't sell you the *sefarim* right now. I am still wearing my *Shabbos* clothing, and I have accepted upon myself the custom to refrain from doing any business transactions while wearing my *Shabbos* clothing, to ensure that I do not inadvertently place money in my pockets and only discover this on *Shabbos*."

R' Zalman looked at the Steipler in dismay. He quickly wrote another note, indicating that his flight back to the U.S. was at five o'clock the following morning, and he would not be returning after *Sukkos*. He would therefore not have another opportunity to purchase the *sefarim*.

"Please allow me to purchase it now," he wrote. "I take upon myself full responsibility to ensure that the Rav will not place any money in his pockets."

The Steipler read the second note, but he explained apologetically that a reminder would not be enough. Since he had already accepted this custom, he could not break it, no matter what the circumstances.

"But I will give you a blessing," the Steipler concluded.

He proceeded to bless R' Zalman and wished him all the best.

R' Zalman, however, was still not satisfied. He racked his brain to come up with a method that would allow the Steipler to sell him the *sefarim*. He couldn't think of anything, but he was desperate. So once again, he wrote a note stating that he would take complete responsibility to make sure that the Rav would not put any money in his pockets.

The Steipler read this third note. He looked up at R' Zalman for a long minute. Then he stood up, told R' Zalman to wait for a few minutes, and left the room.

Two minutes turned into twenty, and still the Steipler hadn't returned. R' Zalman began to fidget. Had he misunderstood the Rav? Perhaps the audience was at an end. R' Zalman was about to walk out the door when the Steipler walked back into the room, wearing his weekday clothing.

The Steipler quickly gathered together the *sefarim* R' Zalman had asked for and handed them to him. R' Zalman took them and paid the Rav for the *sefarim*, marvelling at how far the Rav had gone in order to accommodate another person while at the same time, refusing to bend his custom a single iota.

GUIDING LIGHT

Early in the twentieth century, R' Moshe Yechiel Epstein came to America and settled in the Bronx, New York. Better known as the Ozerov Rebbe, R' Moshe Yechiel built up a legion of loyal followers in America. He wrote the multi–volume works, *Aish Dos* and *Be'er Moshe,* and later moved to Eretz Yisroel, where he was passed away in 1971.

After his death, his grandson, R' Tanchum Becker, inherited the Ozerov dynasty. R' Tanchum founded a *kollel* in Tel Aviv in memory of his holy grandfather.

The *kollel* functioned for 22 years. Eventually, R' Tanchum found that the growing institution needed a new building. A plot of land was purchased in Bnei Brak, and a campaign was started to raise funds for the new building.

The amount of money needed was tremendous. R'

Tanchum enlisted the assistance of his brother in America, R' Leibish Becker, to help him with fund raising. The pressure was enormous, and every avenue of financial resources was tapped.

Almost all of the money had been raised when R' Leibish received an urgent phone call from R' Tanchum. The deadline was coming up, and if the balance wasn't paid immediately, they were in danger of losing the entire building. They were short only a few thousand dollars, but R' Leibish was at a loss as to where he could turn for help.

■ ■ ■

World War II. In America, the draft was in force. Harry Gelb[36] knew that he would be drafted shortly. Instead of getting stuck wherever the army would send him, he decided that it would be best to join the Air Force.

Harry was called to active duty shortly after his paternal grandfather passed away. His grandfather had lived next door to a saintly Rabbi. Before Harry departed for service, his mother decided that she wanted the Rabbi to bless her son. Even though Harry was not religious, he agreed.

Harry and his mother passed through a long, dark hallway before coming to the Rabbi's dimly lit study. The Rabbi lifted his radiant face from the holy books he was studying and listened to their request.

"Of course," he said softly. He warmly gave Harry a blessing for success and a safe return home.

Harry went home, strangely moved by his encounter with the Rabbi, and made his final preparations for the long voyage.

---

[36] *Name is fictitious*

Life in the Air Force was difficult at first. Harry and his fellow cadets were given intensive training, and they had hardly a moment to themselves. But the training proved effective, and soon Harry was ready to join a flight as a bombardier.

Harry and his crew were sent overseas to fly bombing missions over Germany. His crew clicked together right from the start, and most of their missions were successful. Before long, the Air Force recognized the crew's excellent coordination and success rate. They started training them to be the leading crew of future missions.

One day, the entire crew was getting ready to leave on another mission. Harry was startled by a sudden tap on his shoulder.

"The commander wants you," he was told.

Puzzled, Harry went over to the squadron commander. "You wanted to speak with me, sir?"

"Yes, I did. I realize that your crew is going on a flight shortly. But I need to give a place to a flyer who needs this one to finish up his quota. I'm scrubbing you from this flight, and I want you to fly some practice missions."

Harry wasn't too pleased about this. After all, he and his crew were a perfect match. Now he would be behind one mission, and he would need to make it up.

Harry's feelings underwent a quick change, though, when he discovered what happened to his original crew. The plane had been shot down in enemy territory. Those who had not been killed outright ended up as prisoners of war.

Now Harry flew with other crews as a fill–in. In October of 1944, he was sent on a bombing mission to Cologne, Germany. The crew reached their destination, dropped their bombs and were on their way out of Germany. Then disaster struck.

The jarring sound of anti-aircraft fire told the crew that they were being targeted. The pilot frantically tried to turn the aircraft, but he was too late. The plane bucked with the impact of anti-aircraft fire. The pilot fought to stabilize the plane. Two of the engines were destroyed, and now he tried to keep the plane from going completely out of control.

"We're going to try to land in Belgium!" he yelled back to the other crewmembers. "Try to lighten the load in the meantime!"

The other crewmembers frantically threw out ammunition, guns and anything heavy that wasn't absolutely needed. The plane precariously wobbled its way into Belgium. But the power left in the engines simply wasn't enough for a safe landing. Falling short of the American military base, the plane crashed in a nearby field.

Miraculously, Harry found himself unhurt. But the engines were already on fire, and Harry knew that it was only a matter of time before the rest of the ammunition and gas tanks blew up. So he climbed out of the plane as quickly as he could and ran.

As soon as he got clear of the wreckage, he heard calls for help. Looking back, Harry noticed the co-pilot halfway out the window of the cockpit. Flames were visible behind him, and the window was his only means of escape.

The survivors could hear the remaining gunpowder exploding in the plane. But Harry didn't hesitate. He and another crewmember ran over and broke the windows, then pulled the co-pilot out of the plane.

Once again, Harry heard screaming. And again Harry went to the rescue. He found another man, already severely burned, and dragged him clear of the wreckage.

The survivors looked at each other, and then back at the plane, which was now completely aflame. It was incredible they had managed to get out alive.

By the end of the war, Harry had flown over thirty missions and he returned home unharmed. The family was convinced that this was due to the blessings of the saintly Rabbi.

Harry spent the years after the war getting his life back into shape. He married, but he and his wife did not have children for many years. Finally, his mother convinced him to go back to the Rabbi for another blessing.

This time, the Rabbi blessed Harry that he should have a child. And it wasn't long before the blessing came to fruition. Harry's first son, Martin (Moshe), was born a short time later. Two years later, a second son was born.

As Moshe grew up, he was often told stories about his grandmother. His grandmother was involved in raising money for refugees, and she would go to this Rabbi whenever she had any problems in her work.

When Moshe grew older, he became very committed to Torah and *yiddishkeit*. Moshe went to *shul* regularly, and every *Shabbos* he would listen intently to the *rav's* speech. He noticed that the *rav* of his shul would often quote from *Aish Dos*, which had been written by the Ozerover Rebbe.

Moshe found himself greatly inspired by the quotes from *Aish Dos*. One day, he approached his *rav* to ask him more about it.

"Who was the Ozerover Rebbe?" he asked.

"He was a tremendous *tzaddik*," the rav replied. "He lived in the Bronx for many years."

Why do I feel this close affinity to the Rebbe? Moshe wondered. He couldn't put his finger on the source of the spiritual tie he felt to the Rebbe's words.

One day, Moshe noticed the *sefer Aish Dos* lying on one of the tables. Opening it, he discovered that the address of the late Rebbe had been 132 Hoe Street. "Hmm, that sounds familiar," he mused. "Perhaps my father would know more."

Moshe called his father. "Do you remember the name of the rabbi that your mother took you to?"

"No, I really have no idea. I don't think I ever knew his name."

"Well, if I tell you the address, do you think you would remember if it was correct?"

"Could be. What address do you have there?"

"132 Hoe Street."

There was silence on the other end as his father thought it over for a few moments.

"Yes, that's right," he said finally. "That's the house my mother always took me to. Now, how did you know that?"

Moshe explained how he had found the address printed in the *Rebbe's sefer*. "I'm going to find out more about it," he added.

A bit of research told Moshe that R' Leibish Becker was the grandson of the Rebbe. Moshe called him up to ask him for more details about the Rebbe's history. By the time he hung up, Moshe was convinced that this was indeed the Rabbi who had saved his father's life and family.

On another occassion, Moshe called R' Leibish with a personal request. A family member was hospitalized in a rural area, and he needed to find someone to stay with so he could remain near the hospital.

"I'm not familiar with that area myself," R' Leibish told him. "But my brother, R' Tanchum might recall someone from his earlier days in New York who still lives in the old neighborhood. Why not give him a call?"

Moshe called R' Tanchum in Israel. R' Tanchum managed to remember the name of a family who lived only a block away from the hospital. Moshe was able to spend *Shabbos* and *yom tov* in the neighborhood until his family member was ready to leave the hospital.

Time passed. Shortly before *Yom Kippur* one year, Moshe suddenly thought back to his relationship with the Ozerover Rebbe and his family. He decided that after all the help he had received, it was time to show some *hakoras hatov*.

Moshe was not a rich man. But nevertheless, he took out his checkbook and wrote out a check for $1800 for R' Tanchum's *kollel* in Israel, which had been named after the Rebbe. He placed the envelope under the door of R' Leibish's house, and walked away.

Erev Yom Kippur. R' Leibish woke in the morning after receiving his brother's urgent call the night before, no closer to a solution for raising the money. As he opened the door to leave his home, an envelope resting on the floor caught his eye. He opened it up and discovered, to his astonishment, a check for $1800.

R' Leibish called Moshe and asked him for an explanation. Moshe told him the whole story.

When he finished, R' Leibish said, "You have no idea how much I appreciate this check. In your merit, the *kollel* will now be able to purchase its new building. Thank you!"

■ ■ ■

Today, Moshe, his brother, and his father Harry have returned to keeping Hashem's Torah and mitzvos. To them, it is clear that the rebbe continues to pray for them from his exalted place in Heaven.

Holy Counsel

The following story was related by Rabbi Shimon Grama, of Brooklyn, New York and author of The Students Yoman/Daily Planner.

For the first two decades of his life, Tuvia Kadel[37] lived as a secular Israeli. Born and raised in the Holy Land, Tuvia knew next to nothing about his religious heritage.

And then Tuvia joined the growing throng of Israeli *baalei teshuva*. Fired by a deep sense of commitment to Torah and *mitzvos*, Tuvia joined a *yeshiva* and dedicated himself fully to Hashem's service. Just one year after his return to Torah and *yiddishkeit*, Tuvia had already made tremendous strides in his learning and *yiras shomayim*.

But then Divine Providence intervened. Tuvia contracted a life threatening illness, and he grew weaker as the days passed. Friends prayed for his recovery ... but Hashem had other plans. Only a short time later, Tuvia passed away.

His fellow students, his *rabbeim*, all those who had come to know and admire the enthusiastic young man were devasted by the news. But even as they tried to come to terms with their grief, the *rabbeim* in the *yeshiva* were faced with a troubling dilemma. They knew that they ought to visit Tuvia's parents to console them for their loss. Yet they also knew that Tuvia's parents had been furious when their son had become religious. Would the parents even want to see or speak to his *rabbeim*?

Torn by the conflict, the *rabbeim* finally decided to con-

---

[37] *Name is fictitious*

sult with a *gadol*. They went to speak to Rabbi Chaim Kanievsky, the son and successor of the Steipler Gaon.

After hearing them out, Reb Chaim said, "Tell them that in truth, their son should have passed away the year before. But because he became religious, Hashem granted him another year of life to fulfill Torah and *mitzvos*."

The *rabbeim* left in a quandary. No doubt Reb Chaim knew what he was talking about. Yet how could they go to irreligious parents and offer this as a condolence? What did such people know of the power of a *tzaddik* and a *gadol*? Surely they would mock Reb Chaim's words! No, the *rabbeim* decided, they would simply have to come up with a more prosaic way of consoling the parents.

The meeting proceeded much as the *rabbeim* had feared.

"You religious Jews!" the parents said bitterly. "What did our son gain by becoming religious? Nothing! He lost everything, including his life!"

With anger and accusations being hurled at them from all sides, the *rabbeim* slowly realized that none of their carefully prepared remarks were helping. Perhaps, they thought, they should simply say what Reb Chaim had suggested.

"We spoke to Rabbi Chaim Kanievsky about your son," one of the *rabbeim* began cautiously. "He told us that, far from costing your son his life, his newfound interest in religion actually saved his life."

The parents remained silent for a moment. Emboldened, the *rebbi* continued.

"In fact, Reb Chaim said that your son was actually supposed to die the year before and that it was only because he became religious that he was granted another year of life."

There was a sudden gasp from Tuvia's mother.

"It's true!" she yelled hysterically. "Every word the rabbi said is true!"

"You are right," Tuvia's father said, tears streaming down his cheeks. "We blamed you for my son's death, but the rabbi is right. Becoming religious did save his life."

The *rabbeim* simply could not understand it. What had brought about this change in attitude? What was there about Reb Chaim's message that had finally gotten through to Tuvia's parents?

After she calmed down, Tuvia's mother explained.

"Last year, my son began thinking about keeping *Shabbos*, though he wasn't really religious yet. Exactly one year ago, on one *Shabbos* morning, his old group of friends drove up to the house and tried to convince him to go along for some fun. Tuvia thought about it, but he decided against joining them. They drove away, laughing and mocking Tuvia for his beliefs.

"Later that day, the same group of friends were involved in a car accident and all of them were killed. If Tuvia had gone along with them, he would also have been killed. It was his newfound interest in religion and keeping *Shabbos* that saved his life.

"I wasn't willing to admit it then, but deep down I suppose I really knew that religion was helping Tuvia, not harming him. When you told me the rabbi's words, I realized that you were right.

"Thank you. You have consoled us for our loss."

And when Tuvia's *rabbeim* left the house, they went with a new understanding of the faith and trust we must have in our Torah leaders' guidance.

The Right Choice

Mrs. Landers[38] had a problem. She needed to consult a top attorney to help settle a real estate transaction she was having trouble with. But Mrs. Landers wasn't particularly fluent in English. Talking to a lawyer can be difficult even for someone who grew up in America! How would she be able to manage?

After much thought, Mrs. Landers hit on a solution. Why not call Rabbi Shain, the Rosh Yeshiva of Yeshivas Hatalmud in Adelphia, N.J.? Mrs. Landers had seen first hand the genuine warmth and concern Rabbi Shain had for all people during the years her sons had been in his *yeshiva*. Surely he would be willing to help her out now!

Mrs. Landers made the call and put the question to Rabbi Shain. "Would you be able to come with me to meet the attorney?"

"Of course, Mrs. Landers! I'd be happy to help you out."

Mrs. Landers gave Rabbi Shain the name and address of the firm, which was located in Newark, N.J., and arranged to meet him in the lawyer's office.

On the appointed day, Rabbi Shain arrived at the law firm and made his way through the lavishly appointed lobby to the lawyer's office, where he greeted Mrs. Landers.

"Sit down, Rabbi," the tall, blonde lawyer said courteously.

Rabbi Shain sat down and gazed around the office. A quick glance at the diplomas on the wall told him that the lawyer's name was Jonathan Maclay Borman[39].

---

[38] *Name is fictitious*
[39] *Name is fictitious*

"Sounds impressive," Rabbi Shain said to himself. "But something tells me that this man is Jewish."

After the initial greetings, Rabbi Shain decided to pose his question.

"Do you mind telling me if you are Jewish?" he asked.

"Yes, I am," the lawyer admitted. He held up his hand. "But before you get any ideas, Rabbi, I ought to tell you that I am an atheist."

"So how did you decide to become an atheist?"

The lawyer shrugged. "I did go to Hebrew School when I was a child. But the whole experience was disappointing for me. The subjects were boring, the teachers were terrible, and I just became completely uninterested. I considered both sides of the matter, and I made an informed choice."

"Interesting," Rabbi Shain said thoughtfully. "Tell me, do you have any children?"

"Yes, I do," the lawyer said with a smile. "Two wonderful daughters, one eleven and one eight years old."

"And do you send them to Hebrew School?" Rabbi Shain asked.

The lawyer laughed. "Come on, Rabbi. I just told you that I'm an atheist! Why would I send them to Hebrew School?"

"Think about what you just told me," Rabbi Shain urged him. "You became an atheist by choice. You tried religion, saw what it was all about, and made an informed decision. Shouldn't you be giving your children the same choice? By not sending them to Hebrew School, you're forcing them to become atheists. That's not fair, is it? Send them to Hebrew School, and let them decide for themselves, just like you did."

The lawyer stared at him for a moment. "You know something, Rabbi? You're starting to make sense. I'm going to have to think seriously about what you said."

With that, the discussion on religion ended, and they began talking about Mrs. Lander's case. The conversation involved intricate matters of law and diverse subjects, and the lawyer couldn't help being impressed by Rabbi Shain's knowledge of the law, not to mention his common sense.

When the meeting ended, the lawyer remarked, "I really liked some of your ideas, Rabbi. Where did you study law?"

Rabbi Shain laughed. "I never studied law, at least not formally. But my background in *yeshiva* learning and Torah study has taught me never to take anything for granted, until the Torah perspective on the subject is thoroughly researched. This, together with my day–to–day experience in running a *yeshiva*, has given me a wide awareness in many different subjects."

"Well, all I can say is that I'm impressed," the lawyer said with a smile. "It was a pleasure meeting with you."

While the meeting had gone well, Mrs. Landers's case continued to drag on for years. Ten years later, Mrs. Landers had another meeting with Jonathan Borman. This time she brought along another woman to help her out.

In the course of the conversation, the lawyer mentioned Rabbi Shain's name.

"Oh, do you know Rabbi Shain?" the woman asked interestedly.

"I've met him," the lawyer confirmed. "But how do you know him?"

"My son studied in his *yeshiva*," the woman explained.

"Do you still have contact with Rabbi Shain?" the lawyer wanted to know.

"Sure, I talk to him sometimes."

"Then could you do me a favor? Give him a message from me. Tell him that on the same day he spoke to me about sending my children to Hebrew School, I happened to turn on the radio in my car, and I heard a rabbi giving a Torah lecture. I decided that this was some type of Divine Providence, so I contacted a rabbi. Our conversation stayed on my mind until I finally gave my children a fair chance and sent them to Hebrew School.

"Well, they made their choice. They decided to become religious Jews! And they have influenced me to follow in their ways, and I started to attend a weekly Torah class. My life has changed completely, thanks to Rabbi Shain."

A Close Cut

It was 1939. World War II had not yet begun, but everyone knew that it was just a matter of time. In England, the draft was already in force.

One morning, Chaim Michael opened his mail to discover a draft notice. Chaim was not too happy about this. After all, he was from a religious home. How would he be able to keep his Torah way of life in the army? Instinctively, Chaim knew that he would have to resolve to keep at least certain *mitzvos*, no matter what the cost.

One *mitzva* he accepted upon himself was keeping kosher. This proved to be a tremendous undertaking, since even drinking a simple cup of tea could end up being a problem.

The second *mitzva* he took upon himself was not to shave with a razor. At that time, the British were ruthless about appearances. Passing inspections seemed even more important than preparing to fight the enemy. A failed inspection from not having a clean cut shave could lead to a court martial. Chaim did have a hand operated shaver, but he found that it was necessary to shave with it three times a day just to pass inspection.

Late one evening, Chaim discovered that his shaver had a tooth broken. Chaim didn't know what to do. Inspection was the next morning, and there was no way he could pass without his shaver in working condition.

Chaim managed to slip into town, and he began looking for the drugstore owner who lived on top of his store. Eventually, he managed to locate the house. The store was long closed, but Chaim threw some pebbles at the window until the owner finally came down and agreed to let him into the store.

"Let's see," the druggist murmured, as he rummaged through his supplies. "I don't seem to have any replacement teeth for your shaver."

"Oh, no! So what can I do? Do you have anything else that might work?" Chaim was desperate.

"How about this?" The man held up a small tube. "This cream will take off your beard as well as any shaver. Just apply it and wash it off."

"I'll take it!"

Chaim paid for the cream, thanked the man, and made his way back to the army camp. He couldn't wait to try it out.

Back in the bunk, he carefully followed the druggist's instructions. But after one application, nothing had happened. In desperation, Chaim applied the cream a second time and washed it off.

This time something happened, all right. His face felt as if he had a terrible case of sunburn, an itching, burning sensation. One glance in the mirror confirmed that he looked as bad as he felt. Chaim immediately went to the army doctor.

The doctor took one look at Chaim's face and shook his head. "Wow, you really did something to yourself there."

He gave Chaim a cream to soothe the itching. Best of all, though, he excused him from having to shave for seven days. This extra time gave Chaim the chance to buy a new shaver. By the time his week was up, he was all set for the next inspection.

By this time, the war had begun, and the army discipline really began to crack down. Eventually, Chaim was transferred to a different unit that specialized in dismantling mines and other dangerous artillery. Unfortunately, the officers in charge were very anti-Semitic. Chaim found that he had to watch himself very carefully to avoid giving his officers any ammunition to use against him.

One day, one of the officers who often tried to bait Chaim managed to put him on guard command. Not only was this a very difficult task, but on this occasion, it came out on *Shabbos*. Having no choice, Chaim reported to duty unshaven.

The officer was furious. He told Chaim that he would either have to forfeit his corporal stripes or receive a court martial.

Chaim chose the court martial. He was afraid to say that he hadn't shaved due to Torah observance. Instead, he told the court that this type of guard duty usually required three days advance notice. Since he had not received this notice, he argued, he should be excused for coming unprepared.

Fortunately, the court was willing to accept this argument, and Chaim only received a small punishment. Still, Chaim understood that it was only a matter of time before the next episode occurred. He knew that he had to get out of that unit for his own sake. He asked for a transfer, which was granted.

It was only after the war that Chaim discovered how fortunate he had been to be transferred out of that unit. It seemed that the entire unit had been sent to North Africa to dismantle mines, and nearly all had been killed. Thus, Chaim's dedication to keep Hashem's *mitzvos* ended up saving his life.

Of Bagels and Locks

David Greenspan grew up in the Bronx, N.Y., the product of an assimilated American Jewish home. When he reached adulthood, he joined the family's bagel business, which had been in the Greenspan family for generations. After David's father passed away, though, David realized that he wasn't all that interested in bagels after all. He was good with his hands, and he wanted to put them to use.

After taking some evaluation tests, David was told to become a locksmith. He studied hard and soon discovered that he had found his niche. Bagels were out, locks were in, and David soon had a job in the locksmith business.

The pay was good, but David really wanted to strike out on his own. He was constantly on the lookout for a good opportunity, a place where he could establish himself.

One day, David was driving through Monsey, New York. He eyed the layout of the stores in one section of the town. There was a window business there that seemed to catch his eye . . . was this the chance he had been waiting for?

David mustered up all his courage and entered the store to ask if he could rent out a small corner for his new locksmith business.

The store owner was agreeable, and before long, David's new business was setting up shop.

David was now in a very religious area. He figured that the local population would probably make up the majority of his customers, so an ad in a local Jewish circular would be a good idea. He arranged for the ad to be placed, and a few days later, he received his copy in the mail.

David thumbed through the circular until he found his advertisement. "Looks good," he murmured to himself. Absently, David continued flipping through the pages, taking note of the other businesses that were established in the community.

Suddenly a short section at the back of the circular caught his eye. "Lost and Found," the headline proclaimed, and underneath was a series of columns.

David began to read the items listed.

"Found: Gold bracelet. Please call . . . "

"Found: Large sum of money. Please call . . . "

"Found: Diamond earring. Please call . . . "

David couldn't believe his eyes. Were these people actually trying to return such valuable items? And there were so many of them! Whatever happened to "finders keepers, losers weepers"? Here, David saw an entirely different attitude, one based on helping others instead of only taking for oneself.

David figured that if this was what religious Jews were like, it was a group that he wanted to be a part of. Before long, David began to wear a *yarmulka*, and he is now well on his way in his return to his Father in Heaven.

NOT FOR NOTHING[40]

It was a typical morning in the city of Bnei Brak. Rechov Rabbi Akiva was crowded with people, while the traffic behaved in typical Israeli fashion. There was nothing to indicate that this day would be different from any other.

Suddenly there was the screech of brakes. Traffic came to a standstill and pedestrians craned their heads to see what had caused the sudden disturbance. A gasp shook the crowd as they realized what had happened.

It seemed that a woman had started to cross the street, just as a bus turned the corner. And the bus, unfortunately, had not been able to stop in time . . .

The crowd quickly made its way to the scene of the accident. Despite the large number of people, no one seemed to know who the woman was. Her name and address were in her wallet, but she was still unknown.

At that time, the Israeli government allowed autopsies to be performed, often even against the will of the deceased's family. To avoid unnecessary attention by the police, a group of people carried the woman's body into the *shul*, where they hoped it would be able to escape an autopsy.

Hundreds of people were standing in *shul*, reciting *tehillim*, when the police came running in.

"Hand over the body!" they demanded. "We need to release it for an autopsy."

"Why? What do you need an autopsy for? We haven't even been able to contact her family yet!"

---

[40] *This story is related by Rabbi Avraham Tovolsky in his sefer* Sidras Tikun HaMiddos.

The protests came from all sides, and the commotion began to escalate.

Finally the police stormed out of the *shul*. "We'll be back," they warned. "If we need to, we'll take the body by force!"

Someone was quickly dispatched to alert the woman's family, since a family member would have more authority to stop an autopsy. The messenger returned a short while later.

"This woman has no family," he reported. "She seems to have been all alone here."

The group then turned to the local *rabbonim*, who ruled that it was forbidden to hand the body over to the police. "She must be buried immediately with full respect."

A short while later, the police were back, this time in force. As they pushed their way through the crowd, several people approached them and quietly explained that the woman was alone, with no relatives.

"Can't an exception be made for her? Can't she just be buried peacefully?"

Somehow, their words made an impression, and the police agreed to let it go.

Most of the large crowd, which included many respected *rabbonim* and *bnei Torah*, escorted the body to the cemetery, where the woman was laid to rest with the highest respect.

After the funeral, several people wondered what merit this woman had had, to have been buried with such a large and distinguished crowd accompanying her on her final journey. No one seemed to know her. She didn't even live in B'nei Brak!

Finally, one person spoke up.

"I remember this woman from the days of the holocaust in Poland. We were in the same ghetto. I remember how she risked herself for the sake of those who had died in the streets.

She went out into the street alone, time and time again, to give those unfortunate people a Jewish burial. Is it any surprise that she merited this honor today?"

THE FATHER HE NEVER KNEW

Man is the most complex being in existence. Besides his physical intricacies, he has deep emotional and spiritual facets. It would be impossible to ever truly define a person's true nature.

With the approach of Rosh Hashanah and the *Yamim Noraim*, a deep feeling of repentance and introspection had settled over the *yeshiva*. In an effort to share the *teshuvah* mood with the community at large, the *yeshiva* sponsored a public lecture on the topic of Rosh Hashanah and *teshuvah*. The *menahel* asked Akiva Braun, one of the *yeshiva* students and an excellent speaker, to serve as lecturer.

The *shiur* was well attended. The audience, which was comprised mainly of men who were not well-versed in Torah, listened raptly as Akiva spoke eloquently on Rosh Hashanah and the importance of learning Torah. After the lecture, while the participants still lingered in their seats, one elderly man stood up to publicly praise those who devoted their lives to learning Torah.

"Let me tell you," he declared, addressing the entire room. "*Yeshiva* boys are well-behaved, refined gentlemen. They find fulfillment and satisfaction in life. They don't need the escapist worlds of alcohol or drugs; they already have true happiness and contentment in their lives. And this true happiness stems from the Torah itself."

Akiva, impressed by the man's sincere representation of *bnei Torah*, was curious enough to ask one of the other men, "Who is that?"

"That's David Seltzer," the man answered.

Akiva nodded thoughtfully, filing the name away. Then he busied himself shaking hands and making pleasantries to the many laymen who approached to thank him or pose some question or comment about the *shiur*. Time passed, and the entire incident was soon forgotten.

Several months later, as Chanukah approached, Akiva was in the *menahel's* office, waiting to speak with his *rebbe*. The *menahel* was speaking on the phone with the rabbi of the community, and Akiva politely waited for him to finish his phone call.

"*Baruch Dayan HaEmes,*" he heard the *menahel* say. "Who was it? Mr. David Seltzer? I see."

The *menahel* paused for a moment to listen to the rabbi on the other end. Then he spoke again.

"You need boys for *shemirah*? I see. Well, that might be a problem. Chanukah is tonight, and many boys will be away, so I don't really know if it will work out."

Akiva stepped forward. "Excuse me," he said diffidently. "I don't mean to intrude in the *menahel's* conversation, but I think I recognize the name of David Seltzer. If I'm not mistaken, he came to the *shiurim* sponsored by the *yeshiva*."

"Really?" asked the *menahel*. "For a man with respect for Torah, the *bachurim* should sacrifice their time."

The *menahel* thought a moment more. "Akiva, please find out for sure. I can't make up my mind until I know."

Akiva nodded and hurried to the secretary's desk to make a phone call. Minutes later, he turned around and nodded. "I was right," he said. "Not only did Mr. Seltzer come to *shiurim*, but he held *bnei Torah* in very high esteem." He described how Mr. Seltzer had spoken so highly of *bnei Torah* after the *shiur* before Rosh Hashanah.

The *menahel* nodded his approval. "For a *niftar* of that caliber, it is worthwhile. There will be no problem for our boys to help with the *shemirah*."

The arrangements were made quickly. The day was divided into shifts, and different students were assigned to different times. Akiva himself volunteered for the evening shift, eager to do his part to help honor the man who had defended *bnei Torah* so eloquently.

As four o'clock approached, Moshe, one of the older *bachurim* found himself in a nearly empty *beis medrash*. With candle lighting that evening, most of the boys had already gone home. He himself was going first to the funeral home for his *shemirah* shift before returning home. As he left the building, however, he almost bumped into a young man who was dressed as a *yeshiva* student, who was coming inside.

"Can I help you?" Moshe asked.

"Perhaps you can." The other man's face was a picture of the distress. "Is the *menahel* here?"

"I'm sorry, but there's nobody here now at all." Moshe paused at the man's crestfallen look. "Perhaps I could help you?"

"I don't think so. It's in reference to the *levayah* tomorrow."

"Mr. Seltzer's?" Moshe asked. "Are you related to the *niftar*?"

The man nodded and swallowed. "I'm his son," he said, his voice choked with tears.

Moshe cast around for some words of comfort to offer. "Your father bought himself watchmen to do the necessary *shemirah,*" he said finally.

"What do you mean?" the man asked, confused.

Moshe explained, describing Akiva's account of Mr. Seltzer's attendance at the *yeshiva shiurim* and the elderly man's praise of *bnei Torah* right after the Rosh Hashanah lecture.

"When the *menahel* heard about it, it made such a favorable impression on him that he allowed the *yeshiva* boys to undertake the *shemirah,*" Moshe finished. "Your father must have been a very special man."

The man stared at him for a moment, then broke into violent sobs. Moshe, startled, waited for the man to compose himself.

After several moments, the younger Mr. Seltzer told Moshe, "A *rebbe* of mine once contrasted understanding a Torah thought to understanding a person. He said that one could spend days or weeks toiling over a complex Torah subject, and while he may not understand it fully, he will surely come to some degree of understanding. But a person..." The man began to sob again. "A person, even a single Jew, one can never fathom! My own father...I see now that I never really knew him."

Glossary

Glossary

aggadah: homiletic
agunos: women unable to remarry
ahavas Torah: love of Torah
al kiddush Hashem: to sanctify the Name
aliyah: honorary post at the Torah Reading
am haaretz: ignoramous
Aneinu: special prayer added on Fast Days
arba amos shel Halachah: four ells of halachah
aron: coffin
Aron Hakodesh: Holy ark containing Torah scrolls
Aseres Yemei Teshuva: ten days of Repentance from Rosh Hashanah through Yom Kipper
Ashrei: Psalms Chapter 144:15-145:21
askan: community activist
aveirah: sin
avodas haBorei: service of Hashem
avodas Hashem: service of Hashem
Avos: fathers
avreich: married yeshivah

student
baal koreh: one who reads for the congregation from the Torah
baal tefillah: one who leads the prayer service
baal·tekiah: one who blows the shofer
baal teshuva: Penetant
baal tzedakah: A generous person
bachur(im): youth(s)
Bamidbar: Book of Numbers
bar mitzva: ceremony for males at 13, the age at which they are obligated to keep all the Torah's commandments
Baruch Dayan Haemes: "Blessed is the Judge of Truth"; blessing one makes upon hearing of one's passing.
baruch Hashem: thank Heaven
be'ezras Hashem: with God's help
beis din: rabbinical court
Beis Hakeneses HaGra: the Vilna Gaon's synagogue
Beis Hamikdash: Holy Temple
beis midrash: study hall
bentch: to bless
ben Torah: lit. son of Torah, ie. somone who studies and adheres to the laws of the Torah.
berachah(os): blessing(s)
b'ezras Hashem: with Hashem's help
bima: Pulpit
Birkas Hamazon: Grace after meals
bitachon: trust
bittul Torah: waste of Torah learning
bleibt: remains or stays (yiddish)
B'nei Yisrael: Jewish People
Borei Olam: Creator of the world
bris: covenant
chachamim: Torah sages
challah: Shabbos loaf
chag same'ach: "Happy Holiday"
chasan: bridegroom
chassid: righteous person; adverent to Chassidus
chasunah: wedding
chavrusa: study partner

Chazal: Sages, of blessed memory
chazzan: cantor
cheder: elementary Torah school
ches: eighth letter of Hebrew alphabet
chesed: kindness
chevra: group, friends
Chevrah Kadisha: burial society
chiddushim: novellae
Chol haMoed: intermittent days of Pesach or Sukkos
cholov yisrael: Kosher milk; lit. milk supervised by a Jew
Chovos Halevovos: <u>Duties of the Heart</u>; Classic work
chumash: Book of the Pentateuch
chuppah: wedding canopy
Dan lekaf zechus: Judge favorably
daven: to pray
dayan: rabbinical judge
derashah: sermon
din Torah: litigation in rabbinical court
dor hamidbar: the generation that left Egypt and travelled through the wilderness
eishes chayil: a woman of valor
emesdike yid: A ture and pious Jew
emunah: faith
erev Pesach: eve of Passover
erev Shabbos: day before Shabbos (Friday)
eruv: demarcation of private domain
ezras nashim: women's section
frum: observant
gabbai(m): sextant(s)
gadlus: greatness
gadol hador: greatest of the generation
gaon: Talmudic genius
gedolim: great ones
gemach: free loan society
gemara : part of the Talmud
get: religious divorce
gezeilah: theft
gut voch: "a good week" in yiddish
hachnosas orchim: welcoming guests to one's home
hadras panim: a distin-

guished countanance
Hakadosh Baruch Hu: the Holy Blessed One
hakoras hatov: gratitude
halachah: Jewish law
hamotzi: benediction said on bread
Har Sinai: Mount Sinai
HaRav: the Rabbi
Hashem Yisbarach: the Name, G-d
hashgacha: supervision; divine, as in Hashgacha Protis, Divine Providence
haskamah: approbation
hasmadah: diligence
havdalah: concluding ritual of Shabbos
illuy: prodigy
im yirtzeh Hashem: May be the will of Hashem
Kabbalas Shabbos: welcoming the Shabbos
kaddisha: holy; as in chevra kadisha, the holy group (that performs Jewish burial)
Kaddish: mourner's prayer
kallah: bride
kashrus: state of being kosher

kavanah: concentration
kedushah: holiness
kerias haTorah: weekly reading of the Torah
kest: financial support (yiddish)
kever: grave
kevod haTorah: honor of Torah
kibbud: honor
kiddish: sanctification of Shabbos of festival
kipah: skullcap
kittel: traditional white garment
Klal Yisrael: the entire Jewish nation
kohein: hereditary priest
kol tuv: All the best
kollel: Torah study center
Kosel Maaravi: the Western Wall
lashon hara: evil speech
l'chaim: to life
levayah: funeral
Maariv: evening prayers
maasim tovim: good deeds
machzor: prayer book for high holy days and festivals
maggid shiur: lecturer of

Talmud
marbitz Torah: One who spreads the study and observance of Torah
masechta: tractate
mashgiach: supervisor
Mashiach: the Messiah
matzos: unleavened
mazal tov: congratulations
mechutanim: in-laws
melamed: teacher
menahel: principal
mesaddeir kiddushin: wedding officiator
mesiras nefesh: complete dedicaiton
mezuzah: scroll affixed to doorpost
middah: character trait
mikveh: ritual bath
Minchah: afternoon prayers
minyan: quorum of ten
Mishlei: Book of Proverbs
mishnayos: parts of the Talmud
Misilas Yesharim: One of the classic workds written by Rabbi Moshe Chaim Luzzato
mitzvos: Torah commandments

mizrach: eastern wall
modim: Prayer of thanks recited in the morning, afternoon and evening prayers
mohel: Performer of circumcision
mosad haTorah: Torah institution
moser: one who betrays his Jewish brother
Motza'ei Shabbos: night after the Shabbos
muktzeh: something which cannot be touched on Shabbos
mussaf: supplementary service
mussar: ethical instruction
nachas: pride and joy
Nedarim: lit. vows; Tractate of Talmud
Ne'ilah: concluding prayers of Yom Kippur
neshamah: soul
niftar: deceased
olam habaah: World to Come
parshios: weekly portions
pasuk: verse
payot: earlocks

Pesicha: opening as in opening of the Ark in the synagogue
petirah: decease
Pirkei Avos: Ethics of Fathers
poritz: landowner
poseik: halachic authority
p'shat: literal meaning
rav (rabbanim): rabbi(s)
rasha: wicked person
Rashi: Rabbi Shlomo Yitzchoki, famous 11th century commentator
rebbe: Chassidic rabbi or leader
rebbetzin: rabbi's wife
rebbi: Torah teacher
refuah sheleimah: a full recovery
Ribbono Shel Olam: Master of the Universe
Rishon: Early authority
Rosh Beis Din: Chief Justice of Rabbincal court
Rosh Chodesh: first day of Jewish month
Rosh Hashana: The Jewish New Year
rosh yeshivah: dean
sandak: the person given the honor of holding the infant during circumcision
satan: evil angel
schach: special material used to cover the Sukkah
seder: Passover feast
sefer(im): book
sefer Torah: Torah scroll
semichah: ordination
seudah: meal
seudas hodaah: meal of Thanksgiving
se'udas mitzvah: a festive meal celebrating a mitzvah
Shabbos: The Sabbath
Shabbos Hagadol: the Shabbos before Passover
Shacharis: morning prayers
shadchan: matchmaker
shamash: beadle
shanah tovah: a greeting for a good year
Shas: the Talmud
shechunah: neighborhood
she'eilah: inquiry
Shema Yisrael: confession of faith
Shemoneh Esrei: the Eighteen Benedictions

sheva berachos: the Seven Nuptial Blessings
Shevat: Jewish month
shevuah: oath
shidduch: match
shinui hashem: changing one's name
shishi: the sixth person called to the Torah
shiur: lecture
shivah: seven-day period of mourning
shlishi: the third person called to the Torah
shlita: acronym for May He Live a Long and Good Life
shofar: ram's horn
sholom aleichem: greeting, welcome
shomer Shabbos: Shabbos observer
shtender: lectern
shtiebel: chassidic synagogue
shul: synagogue
Shulchan Aruch: Cod of Jewish Law
shver: father-in-law
siddur: prayer book
siddur kiddushin: order of marriage ceremony
simchah: rejoicing
simchah shel mitzvah: the joy of a mitzvah
siyum: celebration
S'na es harabbanus: "Despise the Rabbinate"; ethics of rabbis
sofer: scribe
sugya: Talmudic topic
sukkah: Sukkos booth
taanis: fast day
tallis: prayer shawl
talmid: pupil
talmid chacham: Torah scholar
Tanach: The Scriptures
tefillah: prayer
Tefillah Zakkah: opening prayer of Yom Kippur
tefillin: phylacteries
Tehillim: Psalms
teshuvah: repentance
Tishah b'Av: the Ninth of Av, a fast day
Torah ugedulah bemakom echad: Torah and greatness in one place
Tosafos: early commentary on the Talmud
Tu Bish'vat: 15th day of the

month of Shvat, the new year for trees
tzaddik: righteous man
tzavaah: will
tzedakah: charity
tzidkus: righteousness
tzitzis: fringes
vav: sixth letter of the Hebrew alphabet
yahrzeit: commemorative day
Yamim Nora'im: Days of Awe
yarmulka: skullcap
yeshivah: Torah school
yetzer hara: evil inclination
Yetzias Mitzrayim: the exodus from Egypt
yiddishkeit: Jewishness
yiras Shomayim: fear of Heaven
Yom Hadin: Day of Awe
Yom Kippur: Day of Atonement
yom tov: festival; Jewish holiday
zatzal: Memory of a righteous person is a blessing
zechus: privilege; merit
zeman: semester; term
zemiros: songs
zt"l: see: zatzal

Index of Topics

Index of Topics

DIVINE PROVIDENCE

Hashgacha

Food from Heaven	Vol I, 36
Old York Revisited	Vol I, 48
The Seegasse Cemetery Saga	Vol I, 53
Lost and Found I	Vol I, 56
Way Station to Freedom	Vol I, 60
Saved by the Enemy	Vol I, 124
Entebbi Alive	Vol II, 67
In the Numbers	Vol II, 90
Catalyst for a Car	Vol II, 118
Lost and Found II	Vol II, 122
Reunited	Vol III, 23
Wrong Number	Vol III, 29

Returning Home	Vol III, 31
Special Delivery	Vol III, 35
History Unfolds	Vol III, 38
Divine Mission	Vol III, 40
Shaky Revelations	Vol III, 42
Returned Bread	Vol III, 49
Encounter	Vol III, 58
A Dive in the Right Direction	Vol III, 68

Midah K'neged Midah

Way Station to Freedom	Vol I, 60
By Land and By Sea	Vol I, 65
Care for My Children	Vol II, 116
Computer Match	Vol III, 95
Not for Nothing	Vol III, 194

Small Actions Large Results

Ticket to Eternity	Vol I, 123
Long Term Results	Vol II, 193
On the Right Foot	Vol II, 193

ETHICAL CONDUCT
Forgiveness

The Right Time	Vol III, 133

Kiddish Hashem

The Eyes of the World	Vol I, 45
To Live as a Jew	Vol II, 25
Journey to Health	Vol II, 109

A Moment of Truth	Vol II, 146
A Public Sanctification	Vol III, 64
A Holy Nation	Vol III, 119

Honesty

Advice from the Expert	Vol I, 139
A Word from the Wise	Vol I, 147
Flight from Heaven	Vol II, 131

Shalom

Bakeries and Bar Mitzvas	Vol III, 127

FAITH

Emunah

By Land and By Sea	Vol I, 65
Frostbite	Vol II, 107
Heavenly Reliance	Vol II, 145
Encounter	Vol III, 58
Growing Pains	Vol III, 61

Livelihood

A Loaf of Bread	Vol I, 41
Designated Livelihood	Vol II, 155

Prayer

Of Faith and Prayer	Vol III, 51
Footing the Bill	Vol III, 55

Feelings and Concern

Ahavas Yisrael

To Save a Soul	Vol I, 77
Tears for the Nation	Vol I, 84
Lest Others Stumble	Vol II, 140
A Moment of Truth	Vol II, 146
Concern for Klall Yisrael	Vol II, 143
Sagacious Memories	Vol III, 87
Fatherly Love	Vol III, 97

Bikur Cholim

A Healing Visit	Vol II, 137
Strictly Business	Vol II, 135

Chesed

A Gift from a Godol	Vol I, 86
Marooned in Maine	Vol II, 170
For Heaven's Sake	Vol II, 15
Revolving Kindness	Vol III, 122
A Treasured Handshake	Vol III, 82
Returning Home	Vol III, 31
Good Evening	Vol III, 131

Hachnosas Orachim

Flight from Heaven	Vol II, 131

Nosei b'oil Chavero

A Pair of Boots	Vol I, 75
Some Blood Please	Vol I, 81
Just a Quick Hello	Vol I, 82

Door Dilemma	Vol I, 88
A Scoopful	Vol III, 73
Entrance Exam	Vol III, 78

Nobel Attributes
Admonishment
Admonishment with Love	Vol II, 157
Sagacious Rebuke	Vol II, 158
Mirror Image	Vol III, 100
Bubble Gum	Vol III, 108

Anger
A Run for It	Vol II, 181
Speak Softly	Vol II, 217

Hakoras Hatov
A Catered Thank You	Vol I, 112
Showers of Thanks	Vol I, 114
A Journey of Appreciation	Vol I, 117
Long Deferred Appreciation	Vol II, 101
A Pearl to Remember	Vol II, 163
Revolving Kindness	Vol III, 122
Solid Investment	Vol III, 116

Humbleness
The Secret Formula	Vol I, 101
Surreptitious Sensitivity	Vol I, 105
To Be a Worm	Vol I, 108
Point of View	Vol I, 110

Kiruv
- Long Term Success — Vol II, 149
- On the Right Foot — Vol II, 193
- To Live as a Jew — Vol II, 35
- Reunited — Vol III, 23
- The Right Choice — Vol III, 186

M'vater
- A Blessed Shidduch — Vol III, 113
- A Place Twice Yielded — Vol III, 92

Mitzvohs
Amen
- V'imru Amen — Vol II, 202
- A Diamond of a Lesson — Vol II, 207

Bar Mitzva
- A cup of Inspiration — Vol I, 137

Chanukah
- Chanukah Miracle — Vol III, 154

Covering Hair
- A Mother's Kerchief — Vol II, 126

Hashavas Aveida
- Lost and Found I — Vol I, 56
- Lost and Found II — Vol II, 122
- Of Bagels and Locks — Vol III, 192

Judging Favorably
    Strictly Business   Vol I, 135
    I Was So Sure   Vol III, 136

Mitzva L'shma
    For Heaven's Sake   Vol II, 15

Mesiras Nefesh
    At any Price   Vol I, 130
    Sagacious Attire   Vol III, 174
    A Close Cut   Vol III, 189
    The Angel's Shofar   Vol III, 164

Mitzvah Protection
    Run My Child   Vol II, 208

Mitzvah Goreres Mitzvah
    Mitzvah Connection   Vol III, 166

Minyan
    The Tenth Man   Vol II, 218

Shabbos
    Shabbos Dividends   Vol I, 19
    The Healing Touch   Vol I, 26
    Verdict of the Court   Vol I, 32
    Remember it's Shabbos   Vol II, 80
    To Live as a Jew   Vol II, 31
    Shabbos Radiance   Vol III, 151
    A Public Sanctification   Vol III, 64

Shofar
    The Angel's Shofar — Vol III, 164

Teshuva
    Door Dilemma — Vol I, 88
    Taking Precautions — Vol I, 149

Tzedakah
    His Daily Dose — Vol I, 141
    Short Changed — Vol I, 141
    Donation Deliverance — Vol I, 143
    A Moment of Truth — Vol II, 146
    Tzedakah Incognito — Vol II, 187

Tzitzis
    A Tale of Tzitzis — Vol I, 125
    Mitzva Protection — Vol II, 84
    A Public Sanctification — Vol III, 64

PARENTS - TEACHERS

Chinuch
    The Right Approach — Vol I, 93
    On the Right Foot — Vol II, 193
    Life Support — Vol I, 91

Kibud Av V'em
    A Mother's Gift — Vol I, 68
    A Blessing come True — Vol II, 105
    Anything for a Mother — Vol II, 185
    Family Ties — Vol III, 141

Sages

Blessings
Point of View	Vol I, 110
A Blessing Come True	Vol II, 105
A Blessed Shidduch	Vol III, 113
Guiding Light	Vol III, 176

Foresight
A Cup of Inspiration	Vol I, 137
Of Dreams and Daring	Vol I, 133
A Rebbe's Foresight	Vol II, 213
A Sense of Holiness	Vol I, 150
Holy Counsel	Vol III, 183

Faith in Chazal
A Word from the Wise	Vol I, 147
The Right Doctor	Vol II, 216

Torah

Diligence
A Mother's Concern	Vol II, 198
A Rebbe's Foresight	Vol I, 213
A Priceless Gift	Vol III, 149

Halacha
On the Right Foot	Vol II, 193

Kovod HaTorah
The Father He Never Knew	Vol III, 196